Sly Mongoose

Sly Mongoose

Ken Bolton

PUNCHER & WATTMANN

First published in 2011

Published by Puncher and Wattmann
PO Box 441
Glebe NSW 2037

http://www.puncherandwattmann.com

puncherandwattmann@bigpond.com

National Library of Australia
Cataloguing-in-Publication entry:

Bolton, Ken

Sly Mongoose

ISBN   9781921450303

I. Title.

A821.3

Cover design by Matthew Holt

Printed by McPhersons Printing Group

This project has been assisted by the Australian Government through the Australia Council, its arts funding and advisory body.

Australian Government

Australia Council
for the Arts

"Insouciance, doubt, coffee, a whistled
bit of bop"

— Fassbinder

Contents

2.30

for Alan Wearne, whom "at my back I always hear"

Reading in the dust jacket I see James Schuyler
is 67.

Retsina is my drink
sitting at my desk   2 am

the morning of the day to come
the cool change having arrived

after temperatures of 39 and 43. I slept
early tonight. I slept at *work* today—

& at work last night.
I go there for the cool:

—It's closed: there's no work 'on'—
& use the computer. This year

Rae will be fifty-one.
(Alan told me.) I'll be 42.

Other people's years surprise me more.
I know my own.

Though I forgot—thought I was forty
for quite some time. I must

ring mum.

(What for, to ask my age? No,
to say hullo.)

All of this unhurried—I
sense no *ticking*.

The poems of Schuyler catch time as movement, as
fluid, graceful, beautiful—

and quick.

They don't suggest much *agency* I guess.
I am not going to judge him.

My mother. I wonder how
she is. We are not close.

I have not seen her much since I was eleven.
Probably I love her anyway. (Surprise, surprise.)

She is light, & blonde, & physically maybe
not tenacious. I don't want her

to be ill. She dresses in beige, & nougat,
whites—

I wonder if she is an *Air* sign?

I could go & find
one of the women's magazines around the house

& see what sign
January is.

I want her to live forever.

My dad is more substantial. I don't
want him to die either—

but because I see him more,
I can see it coming. *My* body,

perhaps, is more like his. There is
no basis in this.

One time I sat behind her in the car.
An extraordinary number of facial gestures

& things she did to her
face, with her hands,

were mine exactly.

I hear Michael come down the hall
& out the front door.

This means he is standing, looking
across the road—where *I* see

only dark, an indistinct road sign, the sense of leaves,
& some gleam from a car. I say

"Hullo Michael,"
in case he is there—& he comes round to my window,

naked, his body warm & brown
holding a towel & a glass of water.

He is nice.

We say some usual things, & he goes back to bed. "Having a bit of a
write?" he asks.

I say, "Yep.
Nice when it comes."

The expression theory of art.

No comment. Or, that *was* a comment.
And comment enough.

I am glad to be doing it.

Michael's mother
is ill. And James Schuyler's mother

died, in one of the later poems.
I am

'of that age'.
I guess. Though

I have always been interested in time. *The time
is now*—I look over my shoulder, at the

Public Service clock, stolen for me
by Gary Oliver all those years back—I just

put batteries in it this morning—it's said nine
o'clock for months now—*2.30.*

Letter To Akira Back In Japan

—the gossip, the identity question, etcetera

> "The distance between
> me & Japan
> is like that between
> a frog — & a cell
> telephone"
> > — Akira Akira, in an email

> You Can Never Go Home Again — Look Homeward,
> Angel — You Can Always Go Back — Don't Look Back —
> He Never Returned
> > — various authors, *The Literature of Exile*

What a great email to get.

I'm sorry this has been

     SO LONG coming to you.

        Every day, I think

Make that reply!

If I hadn't kept fantasizing

        a terrific,

long,

  & personal letter

     you'd have had it sooner.

    Better, too, maybe

So,

  There You Are,

      turning

Japanese,

turning Australian.

("Turning Japanese"

a pop song

not long ago)

But *all* artists

(they say)

are in

"permanent internal exile".

So why not you?

— Or is that only poets? —

(Or is it a *notion*, only—
only a notion—
that poets like ...

about themselves

INDIVIDUALLY,

other poets ...

are part of the problem
— the background
against which you stand out.   ?

Is it like that for artists?)

*

Well, 25 years at Gulag EAF —

the aesthetic salt mines!

And you want to 'join' ?!
Well, welcome, brother,

here's your pick, here's your shovel.

Your 'frog-&-
phone' image:

the 'disconnect'
between you & Japan.

Funny.

I wonder where could *I* live—
apart from here?

Maybe Ireland (?)

—but the weather,
Jesus.

Hey,

have you started swearing in Australian?

No, not 'Fuck', that's universal —

You should try Jesus!

\#

I remember a friend of mine

instructing an Englishmen
on the best way to enter a railway carriage,
here,
travelling intersate:
you walk in,
glare about you
hurl your bag
in the corner of your
seat, shout *Fucking
government!*

                     & sit down

                              glowering

                #

So, stay another year?

                  FOREVER?

'Indefinite' is best —

                      that can *be* forever

                              without sounding
                                   like

                            a sentence.

          (*He Never Returned.*

            Don't Look Back.

               Etcetera.)

                #

the disconnect

#

But have you thought
Japanese strengths might be working for you:

determination?

a wish to succeed, in the face of

difficulty?

The denial of pain?

Stereotype. Right?

I mean,

are you calmer,
focused, more
balanced'—
than the other nutters out there?

#

Just
an outsider

with your mind
on the game.)

#

That is, "just an
outsider with

consequently
Your Mind On The Game"

#

You needn't worry
about being

permanently
an 'exotic'.

(Though 'a figure
of some romance'? —

Useful? Weird?)

So stay.
The place

would seem weird
without you.

#

If you went back permanently
would you be part of the debate there

— that everyone/no-one is
having?

(No one is invited
to the debate here,

except

Greg Sheridan
Janet Albrechtson.)

\#

the minions of Murdoch

Rupert's minions

\#

Speaking of News Ltd—
There is none:

no news:

I've mostly been doing
bookshop stuff & proofing EAF articles,

& began (finally,
on Saturday, a week after I thought I'd be on to it)

the small essay for Sarah's show
at the 'Eaf'.

> Which, as you
> know—
> Rhymes with "leaf"—

I finish it tomorrow.

My main worry
(the 'news' continued),

was another essay —
written on the basis

of a studio visit
& J-pegs.

Anyway, I struggled with it for ten days —

after writing a bad,
lumpy beginning.

Then, when I'd left it as late as possible,
I got started —

& had a horrible four or five days on it ...
And *sent it to them lumpy*

— but with an invoice!

So,
went to Peter McKay's DOWNTOWN show.

                                        Good
to see DOWNTOWN
                          treated like an opportunity —

not just the standard two pieces
                                    intimating, strenuously,
                                    as they usually do

that the artist
                is   'not trying too hard' —

                                    three distinct (small)
'bodies' of work.

On the other hand,

Was the work
so good?

But we'll see more of him.
Best were photos

of what looked like night sky: myriad
stars in whorling clouds,

against an ink-black background.
These,

as you may already know,
were pix of oil slicks,

in car parks around town,
to which Peter had added glitter, & surface fixative.

        (I was reminded

                 of the pix of

urinals

      in the CAC's Scott Redford show

            a few years back —

that is, I could imagine these being
          nearly that good to look at:

but without the irony & complexity
      —I guess the meanness —
            we associate with 'grown-up'.

           It was just that
'stars-in-the-gutter' conundrum —

which doesn't mean much — after

1880?

1930?)

(Or is it perennial?)

(Does it always
mean something to someone?)

\#

But I liked them.

\#

Festival of Ideas last week: Melentie & I
walked to Fiona Hall's opening —

& got dragged

to the nearby Festival's launch
(Not my idea of fun —

& not Melentie's—
exhausted,

after a week of being ill,
then a trip to Brisbane, to

talk to artists.

He was moving so slowly — & was so pale —
I might have offered to carry him,

at least up the hill
& past Parliament.

But he's bigger than I am!)
So,

a night of speeches, with all
the good & bien-pensant & well-heeled

holding glasses.

(Have you noticed
the amount of French in this?!

Clearly,
I'm out to impress.)
The best part
was when

Miss Mandy asked,
in an effort at conversation,

if I were going "to very much
of the Festival?"

& I was able to answer, with singular brightness,
None!

She'd not bargained
on

'the wrong set' showing up —

& from a world
'so near her own'.)

#

Fifi's show
was okay:

but her work
loses something en masse.

(At any rate, it invites — or 'inspires' — the question
Why not stop?)

(It invites — or 'inspires' — the shout
Please desist!)

The things made of soap
were really nice.

If you're back soon...
you'll have missed nothing.

#

I wonder if you will tell me about Japan. Ever.
I mean, will I ever 'find out' about Japan?

How to get a complete picture?

I like
the 'idea'
of the place —

where I figure, however, I'd be
a fish-out-of-water

(or is that 'telephone'?).

(Today, Tuesday morning,
I've begun this poem to you.

My usual pace
might mean …

dot dot dot

But great to be writing something!)

Do I sound a bit grizzled, do you think, & a bit,
melodramatically,

the bohemian class-warrior
in
this email/this
poem?

— Honest, Judge —

I don't know
What Came Over Me!

I don't know about turning this
into a poem, either — though Then You'll Have

My Full Attention. Or will
the poem have it?

ha ha.

The gap between you and most of
Japan

resembles that between frog & mobile phone!

I remember feeling the same

about me & Hornsby (!)

(& disapproving of myself as I did).

Adults wandering past, tubbily,

in shapeless, gelati-coloured
clothes, fit for children

(I was twenty,
& had read a lot of novels.

I didn't want to be a snob —
but 'Australian suburban life'

looked awful.)

If I spoke Italian ... & had gone to Italy

aged thirty,

I could've married an Italian girl!

But then

you sort of become gradually Italian —

& the *point* is to stay who you are,

definition given

by your difference
from all around you

& definition given,
too, to all you see,
& think —

that's if Existential Truth, the agony
of consciousness,

        is for you.

Do you
live with that?

I live with it all the time

        — in my heroic way,
over coffee, reading, writing

        (art criticism, a letter ...

            to friend Pam,
            or Laurie,

                a letter to you).

                      #

                        As

                the Japanese person I know
                    best

— well, the only one —

        how can I
        learn about Japan
        if you won't be true to type? Huh?

           — good joke? —

              Or,

be like me, at least,
since we're friends.

(The frog-&-phone scenario, see?
                        — the *only* one, for the *poèt
                                  maudit.*

Ring ring! Picks up frog — hullo?
A voice barks, *Wrong end! Wrong end! Wrong end!)*

(Maxwell
Smart)

(Turns frog around —
taps it on the head.)

(Hullo?
Chief?)

You don't seem
like an 'artist maudit'.

                       (Why, where's your
                       alcohol problem,
                       your pensive air?)

You don't seem like
an Existentialist, either

                  — if Juliet Greco was an Existentialist.

(You'd find her, maybe,
rather dowdy —
                  tho Jean-Paul Sartre,
                        that one-eyed masher,
might have felt her charm ... —

all that smoke, the coffee,
the bongo drums)

(Juliette probably had *her* eye
on someone younger.)

For an Existentialist
I guess your 'air' is about right.

Tho I see you
'in colour',

        whereas Existentialists are black-&-white.

Oh-oh, here comes Juliette Greco —
Look the other way!

      You could meet the people you have to read now —
      meet them *young* — Jacques Lacan

        over there, at that table, a study in bottled rage

and there's a shy Althusser
& Deleuze is buying a drink

—for Juliette Greco!
to Sartre's disappointment,

      & Simone's grim approval.
      & look, there's Yves Montand.

This is a story-book Paris.
Which Simone do I mean, for example? —

   both!

Have I spent my life
calibrating the 'New York' — 'cosmopolitan', or 'Roman',

or at least 'sophisticated' —

response to things,

& mentally applying it
here,

in Hindley Street?
(after years
in Rundle),

a sophistication
I knew nothing of

outside of books?!

Ten years before the mast /
Of Caffeine!

The lash /
Of vigilant concentration!

You at least have got
further out

on a more literal limb:
here you are — with
"tramps like us"
(Lou Reed)

"bozos like me"
(Kenzaburo Oe).

\#

"You know,"

(spits in grass, heaves sigh,
squints eye at the sun)

"there's been
many a time

— fighting the good fight
perusing the difficult texts

daydreaming etc —
imbibing my

existential coffee,
when I've derived

Crucial Extra Strength —
from the sign you made

that I stuck on my glasses-case: *our friend ken* …"

though you hardly know me
        (Ray Charles)

                "And I aint forgettin'—
                No sir, I aint forgettin'!"

((Know that movie?))

But we're friends, I think —
& (like all here) I'm moved

that someone smart as you

wants in.

> I'll move over a bit: you can see
> where I've been chipping.

> See, how the coal — the aesthetic coal —

breaks away occasionally:
> That's progress, right?

> And you say, *I thought it was salt we're after.*

Stay on track, Ken!

> Ken

> PS You like the way
> I did that —

"Ken / Ken",

AkiraAkira?

Say hi when you're back!

Note: Akira Tamura is known in the Adelaide art world as Akira Akira, a
sarcasm halving the number of repetitions he must make in giving his name.

Guillaume Apollinaire

"amply repays the debt to O'Hara
and through him to Apollinaire"

David Malouf

In the park, as I stroll along, I see a man who looks
like Apollinaire—that head shaped like a pear, a garlic,
as in the small drawing of him by Picasso, wherein
Apollinaire is depicted as the pope. I doubt that it is
him of course but cannot resist going near. It is him.
He thanks me for fully repaying my debt to him 'after
all these years'. *When*, he asks, *will John Forbes pay? I
mean fully*, he says, when I look at a loss for an answer.
"What about Pam?" I ask.

       Pam Brown? He shakes his
head slowly, *No*. I take it she *hasn't* paid. She has just
been to France, she could have called by the tomb. I
have not spoken, but Guillaume Apollinaire appears to
have read my thoughts. *No*, he nods, sadly.

"Hey!" I say, "I'm a friend of theirs. How's about a
drink, to maybe repay you?" We go to *Zorbas* and
drink retsina. Later, to the *Cargo Club*, a late night
bar, where we go as the restaurant closes. I practically
have to carry him—but it'sjust across the street. "There
must be so many," I say, thinking of all who must owe
him. *Yes*, he says. So far he has spoken not in French
but with a French accent. *Yes*, he agrees, sipping, his
beret on the table. "And none of them have come by?"
I am incredulous. *From here?* he asks—& offers, *Alan
Wearne*. "Alan?" (I am surprised.) *And he owes me
nothing.*

He came to see the tomb of Van Morrison, he adds after a
time. "Jim," I correct him, quietly. *Please,* he says, *call
me Guillaume.* The salad is terrific. And the sardines
look really nifty—sort of 'School of Paris', I point out.
Apollinaire says, *Yes—like Soutine on an orderly day, or
Braque.* The bread is really fresh. I say, "Surely so many
poets owe you something. It must add up. Better not to *wait*
to be repaid, it can only get you down. Better to be pleased
at it!" At this he smiles and ducks his head, guiltily amused
and we really get to drinking.

Art History

for Gregory O'Brien & Ernst Gombrich

"Art History, you box on regardless"

Ah, Art History, you are
multifarious,

like overcoats
on a hall stand at a party

resembling each other, but different—

& a taxi calls—but which is
yours? the taxi is
but which art history, which art-historical coat?

Something raffish, & worn,
& scoundrelly about the collar—winks, or shrugs

— like Gully Jimpson, Colin
McCahon—a little frayed—

or Max Jacob (as played
by Roy Rene—for this is not
Art but Art History) —

& you pull it
from the others, & it is yours &
you race to the taxi & the taxi
races you, from the party you were at
to the party you were going to.

The cosy, rather battered coat
that is your art history

—the history-of-art *for you*—

fits
not too snug but snugly,
ah!

In it whole periods are truncated,
take disproportionately
less time or space
than they needed in real life

—or they happen only '*here*' or '*there*'—

nothing you don't know exists (note
the bit of sticky tape
that adheres to the back of your coat

—adheres to your coat, sure,
but at the back, unseen—

                                        or the lining
that, similarly, hangs behind.

—A little ragged, but who's to know? Others,
that's who—you don't.
An avant-gardist, you face
resolutely forward).

                In this History
some maintain presence by an
invincible right to be there,

despite your willed blindness—

like your rivals in a share house.
You come grudgingly
to love them,
& to know them with
perhaps more justice.

"Pass the butter, Pablo."

Of all people, Picasso is one.
I loved Braque. I will always
love him more. Though,
undeniably, Picasso's pictures, often, are just 'greater'—
greater, that's all!

                    The Renaissance,
for me, is 'totally Italian', until
I remember Durer—by whom I am
'much struck'.
                    But then the word exerts
its Italianate pull, & I think again
of Perugino, & Leonardo …
of Piero di Cosimo, & the Davids & Saint
Georges & Madonnas that abound.

                    I liked
Andrea del Sarto (like Braque)
more than I should—

& Pontormo & Parmigiano
at least as much as I should
(others less so),

                    & Annibale Carracci
I felt curiously defensive of—&
feel so still!

Caravaggio perhaps
("perhaps"?) led to more, was 'greater', yes—
but his pictures are often cold, where

Annibale, at his least World-
Wrestling-Federationy best,

can be looked at for longer: the softer
more humane vaguery of his line
does not repel.

(*St Margaret* and *The Rest
on the Flight into Egypt*—
is that what it is called?—
might make my point, my not
very substantial point.)

        The Baroque, I feel,
I often loved,

         though not the idea of
the Baroque.

        Guido Reni I saw
when I visited Paris was
mostly a dud, but
Domenichino—

(I saw in Rome—
confirming a prejudice
I had forgotten almost I had)

was great—

viz his *Communion of St Jerome*.

I was taught the Baroque, long long ago,
by a German nut,

whose tutorials I cut
& whose lectures —thud   sigh—

regularly put me to sleep.

I worked long hours
as a nurse's aide
in an old folks' home

& Sydney Uni's early morning start
saw me, always, in the preliminary rounds,
down for the count—

as Wilhelm rambled on, desperately—
speaking of the p'sooch-o-logical effect of this
& the spirit-oo-arl aspect of that

& we looked on, at a faded slide of Altdorfer.

I cared so much I did well.
Rembrandt I cared about,

& Titian. I care about Rembrandt still
but Titian more—& the Venetians, like Tintoretto,

I like now more than I did then: I have
out-grown my Art History, as I've met

the real thing—whole new extensions &
verandahs made, in the light

of meetings with this actual art,

though the unrenovated sections of the building
—the museum of my Art History—while fictional,

are solid enough, though admittedly
visited less & less.

Phantom limbs
whose toes & fingers
I never wriggle now.

Sometimes I walk
into these rooms

& it is as if I have
stumbled upon 'charades'—

& an old scene I ought to
know but don't—

                    (but am
I really exploring a building?
I thought I was wearing a coat?)—Viz.,

There is Mr Moreau (Gustave),
sternly, or chastely, painting—before the Fauves,

who ignore him
& toil away *less* chastely, more manfully, more cheerily—

respectively, Matisse, Vlaminck, Dufy—

but a little impressed nonetheless,
a little 'influenced',

that is my theory. Though only Roualt
knows he is influenced.
                    Too bad for Gustave.

Ah, the French,

the French tradition:
Poussin, Chardin, Ingres,

Derain, Balthus,
Jean Dubuffet—

petering out with
Fautrier & Soulages,
the repetitions of Giacometti.

It was probably real angst,
to give him credit.

But I don't credit it—
give me, any day, Maillol!

Which takes us back to Poussin,
perverse nut, whom the world, perversely,

learns to love: the grace, the
stilted artificiality! (Better

that he *was* Poussin, than
another, paler version of Venice.
                              Right?)

The Titian in London's
National Gallery made me
weep, it was so
terrific, so daring, *The Death
Of Actaeon,*
                 as if Titian
were suddenly possessed
by Tony Tuckson (in an era

it would have been so much harder
to *be* Tony Tuckson in). I read later

it had been too drastically cleaned
in gallery restoration.

Tragic, unsettling thought!

Art History's revenge on real art,
this practical revisionism.

What to think—
(I felt that feeling; the tears
were involuntary,
if 'produced' by thought
or theory: I.E.,
I was *prepared* to shed them,
for that Titian,
softened up) ?

*

It's a conundrum.

And here, towled down,
mouth-guard rinsed & replaced,
Art History must breathe deeply
& be prepared to box on.

*

And there is the history
of Art History to consider—

those dud mistakes
& scandals of the past:

Duveen—but, better,
the more genuine mysteries:

Constantin Guys, Anton Mengs,
the puzzling taste

of times long gone.

Who painted
Loves For Sale? (Vien.)
(I remember, sometimes, to my surprise.)

Someone
held it 'vulgar' back then, ha ha.

Jacques-Louis David
is an interesting figure, the art

—alternately, almost picture by picture
(depending what book you're looking in)—good,

bad, wrong-headed, homely,
bizarre,

knockout.

But Modernism, you
were my friend, & love, & inspiration—

replacing rock'n'roll in my mind as
a register, a palimpsest, an abacus or braille,

of moves, escapades,
great feats, ripostes, endgames,

breakthroughs & breakouts, the screw
twisting inevitably tighter

—starting somehow with Manet
but retrospectively taking in Watteau,
Poussin (!), &, against his wish,

Ingres: *"Must I sit? then I will sit over here"*—

chooses stuffed Louis Quinze chair
in corner, *averting his head*—

from the Douanier Rousseau, Utrillo,
Cassat & Laurencin,

the raffish Picasso, & the calmly
lunatic Marinetti, &,

say, Ernst, & Miro?
He finds his eye

caught
by de Chirico's noble bearing

& tears it away—*"Neither am I
that sort of nut,"* he says,

but accepting, as he does, an accommodation,
wondering *"Where is Delacroix?"*

                         What weird enthusiasms
I have had, in my time, Art History,

will have again perhaps—
but less, I think, under your influence.

                    Emile
Nolde I once liked.

It didn't last, replaced
by a sudden grasp ...

of the urgency, & accuracy,
the angrily abridging, & cuttingly summary,

line—of Ernst Ludwig Kirchner.
Right for once!

Outside of books & slide lectures
it seems he really is great. Even outside of them!

                    August Macke
was a one-time enthusiasm—

not that I can't see why,
but 'not very complex'—

Bellini I liked (& who could not like
Giorgione?)—Watteau I loved &

love still; Tiepolo, & Guardi (Ti-
epolo I now like 'better', but
picture by picture—
                    & Guardi seems
a wrong enthusiasm: in the flesh
the colours too saturated, intense);

Chardin, yes, & Rembrandt's drawings—
almost separately, *additional* to the paintings—

are terrific, a gift to us, testimony
to the quick human eye of another time,

babies stumbling & toddling
hands held out, dogs sniffing,

& something like 'street life'—
the human shuffle, mundane

& loved, their various limps
& rolls & swaggers

or quick, light steps, their
jollity, severity, hope

as they perform these manoeuvres.

Manet was great.
It is almost hard to imagine

what kinds of awareness can have handled
the pressures, & currents & intuitions

that seem to have passed through him:
the actual, the modern,

a politicized, class-conscious
formalism
            (the girl & her mother
by the train station, each in their
different, mental space,

                          the daring
confrontational, didactic stare
& the 'Mme Recamier',
Venetian-odalisque pose

of the prostitute,
with maid & cat—the coat-trailing
mimicry

of the three picnickers—
the men &
nude girl
                    (& the girl
at the stream, further back):

What is wrong with this picture? Manet asks,
pretending at 'guilelessly')—

how can you not love that,
or the small flower-piece still-lives,

a rose floating chill-ly
in water & cut glass, a camellia?

He is too great. (I think "Walter Benjamin"
& look out this café window at 'modern life'—

two male figures under an orange umbrella sit—
in blacks & greys Manet's palette
would have registered exactly,

both on mobile phones.

Seconds later they laugh, one man's
bald head & glasses reminding me

of my art-critic friend Michael Newall, this guy's
orange loafers, tho, 'not quite Michael'; the chairs

are Marie Laurencin pinks, aquas, & lemon colours,

the vine above them saying 'Italian',
but equally almost, 'French'.

It is Australia.
The birds that hop there now,
picking crumbs, are local—

though Dufy might have captured them
or Carel Fabritius, or Datillo Rubbo, or Michael Fitzjames.)

Picasso, Matisse—the Americans.... .
One resisted the level of hype,

but Pollock really was terrific
many, many times—& Warhol ... the list

trips off the tongue.

Rauschenberg I liked,
in *books*, fatally, better than when I see him.

The minor figures—whom I loved for being outside
Art History—I love still: Joe Brainard,

Caulfield, Tuckson, Fairweather, Crowley ...

•

Examining you, Art History
—not the house, the coat—I find

pieces patched, & mended &
altered, whole new arms

sewn on—*what kind of octopus ...?*

—Kirchner is, here
—the what?—the favourite lapel,

a lapel looking better, now, than it ever did

—or am I changing coats?

or changing the overcoat
that was Art History,

for the more functional sports jacket, of real art?

Art History has 'left the building'—

or have I left the building Art History was—with its
weirdly added rooms, false doors, rooms there was
no entering ("The Baroque in Prague" for example),

to be wandering down the street & into
a gallery, or an artist-run space or someone's studio—

or am I merely
having coffee, thinking about what I saw

& what I haven't seen? Is this 'Art History' *again*

—a new, a better coat? By 'another name'—
old loves, burnished like Kirchner?
& the relegated, exiled,
excised (like Otto Mueller? — yike!)?

& new adornments added: Weegee, de Pisis,
Ryman, Kiefer... Polke   ?   Is it? Huh?

     ... the works reappear in real life & are
still great—if not *so* great—or are greater than,

proportionately, I had habitually ranked them—

                they survive
to say a cheery *boo!* here & now—

which makes them heroes, survivors,
wise jokers—whose practical joke

is to turn up, real, actual,
amazing.

        De Chirico!
I am almost over

my decades of enthusiasm *for* you, amusement
at you (for being sometimes

so absurd, often at the
same time as great—

at other times absurd only
—but proudly, sternly absurd, obdurately):

Yet when I see you you get my vote.

Bonnard, Vuillard? *Certainment!*
Robert Morris—

those boxes, not so great really!

Bladen, *The Big 'X'.*
I'll always love you.

(Though this is 'Art History':
I have never seen you in real life!),

("There will always be Art History."
Fact?)

                                        Sir,
the waiter says, *you appear to have spilled
your coffee—all over your sleeve!* looking at
my fourth, my fifth arm, doubtfully (it's
a funny-looking coat), *Your taxi is waiting.*

I open the door throw the coat in & plunge in
after it.

"To the conference, sir, with the art historians?"
pipes the driver who resembles

Roy Rene or Keenan Wynn

or sad-faced Tony Hancock
dressed as an artist on his day job—

Drive on! I say, & settle back
& we drive off. *"Tell me, gov—
our DESTINATION?* [He looks around] *Um,
is that your 'Art History' coat?"*

—the extra sleeves,
the disjunctly placed pocket—

                        He has me picked:

I guess I am going to the Conference—
of Art Historians—

to 'share views'

Art History, you are like a museum
in the mind, a museum

in each art historian's mind,

one in which we are
the director & curator,

the researcher,
the education officer,

& approving, approving audience

                And Art Criticism ... (the subject
of another poem), *you too I love!*

—tho I refuse to see a
distinction, a firm one:

let no one try that formulation
"properly speaking".

Maybe in truth I have always been an amateur:

Wouldn't it be great? & *Isn't it great?* being, respectively,
my versions of

Art History & Art Criticism?

My heart has lifted so often
at their works
& many others'

that I wonder what
other people think about—
sport, religion?

(I guess it is the fashion—a girl gets up
from that same table the guys sat at:
suit, pants, brief-case—"the heroism of
modern-day life"

       —that Caillebotte
could have caught exactly.) Is this
a manifesto, a confession,

a monument
that would list the great dead—
or all these things?

How much better
to have been an artist—

than a politician, a soldier

(though many a
fallen soldier, I know, would have agreed.

Some, I suppose, wouldn't.
Peace!)

The funny names:
Orthon Friez, Kees
Van Dongen! (Cy Twombly.)

The Greats: Manet,
Cezanne, Lautrec,

Picasso & Braque

Bonnard,
Matisse. Kirchner,

Beckmann—Gorky
Pollock, Duchamp,
Warhol … Beuys & the coyote,

        the art of
my own time & space—
Micky, Shaun & Bron',
Kurt Brereton.

Should I take off this coat?
or wear it 'lightly', continental-style,

over my shoulders?

To all on this too short list—
Anton, Otto,

Edouard, Bronwyn—my salute!

Brisbane Letter To Gabe

Sydney, in the paintings, negates all—

views
that pre-date & outlive the viewer.

A Sydney of the past,
of now, & extending past your time:

there are ten million stories in the Naked City,

yours makes
no difference.

Dear Gabe,

      I'd like to write you a poem.
I should write you something—

a letter—but what's to say?
Hanging about together would be best.

I often get the sense, when I begin this way,
of the addressee—standing—as if challenged to a duel,

indicating they are in no way armed, & unable to reply.

On the other hand, who better to think aloud to
than you, pal? Permission granted?

(You know that Italian phrase—I love it—that goes "permesso"—
usually to hand you something you need—a knife, a fork?

Maybe a letter is what you need.)

I read Peter Schjeldahl's review
of the Picasso-Matisse show yesterday—

that we saw, six years back, at Tate Modern.

It's a great review.
I should send it to you.

Reading it, I was suddenly back there.
We did some hanging around that night.

We ate somewhere, I guess, & sat thru that movie,
Rififi, that I recommended.

Of interest
(inverted commas) but a dud.

And then at midnight the Tate.

I feel, sometimes, when I look at real art, that I've
let that game go— it's

got away from me,
is not part of my life. Then I forget

& go back
to thinking about art.

I'd see a lot more
if I lived closer to it.

But, here, Adelaide, now—
I *think* I'm thinking of going to bed.

"That was a short one," I hear you protest—
"an avowal—then an

early retirement."
Night, on the other hand, late,

is the time
to start these things. And I've started this.

A sudden burst of activity,
an attempt to keep the brain alive.

The pilot light, about to go out.

My coffee cup—small & red-&-white—
catches my eye, sitting on its saucer, on an old green copy of

From Here To Eternity
Cath bought me. It winks & looks

jauntily hilarious, the cup.

"Eternity can wait!" the cup says.
"Eternity can wait *if I can*"—because

it is not usually there
that I'd leave a cup,

where it sits very provisionally,
waiting to be knocked, or overbalanced.

I'll never read it,
the James Jones book,

but its lettering looks so dramatic—

white out of a deep,
spinnachy green—why Cath got it.

The Agony & the Ecstasy, Lust For Life.

Of those titles *Some Came Running*
is my favourite.

It is good in a joke.
(I often hear it in Mary Christie's voice—

offered as an amused corrective...)
but I like it on its own terms, too.

It says "Stay up!
Don't quit!"

Like my cup.

I make a hot water bottle, & put it
for a second

out of habit

on Cath's side of the bed—
but Cath is in Hobart,

on Bruny Island.

I've never used a hottie before:
they seem to *distract* the body

from the initial cold.
(Even, "distract *merely*".

Though I'm not sure.)

I wonder
what it's like over there?

London, not Tasmania
(where it'll be freezing—Cath's friend Lorraine

rang, told me). It's past the time
of record temperatures, heat-waves, now, in England. Yep?

They're not making the news here.
The war in Georgia, the Olympics,

keeping it off the screens? No, there is always time
for a few shots—of cars freezing on the motorway,

snow shovelled—

or people bathing in the Trevi Fountain,
pale skin in Hyde Park.

        Twelve or so weeks
& you'll be here, right? Mid, or late December?

Thus escaping the UK cold,
its sharpest spike. Compensation—*for all that travel*—

just to attend your
friends' weddings.
            Meanwhile
     (I don't know where you'll read these—

     in the sun outside?
     on your way to work?),

here are some poems
I wrote recently—written

in a funny mood.
I decided to just 'make myself write'

ready or not. So they
come out inconsequential as always, but less studied.

Is it the high pondering
that indicates the ambition

for 'high art'?

These don't have it.
That's something.

Cath fixed the Bruny Island trip

months ago.
I arranged for Brisbane in February or March.

It turns out they overlap.
So Cath does a week on Bruny & I fly out

an hour or so
before she gets back.

Four or five days in BrisVegas, as
Chris calls it (Anna's

boyfriend, whom I think
you'd like). Yes, other people call it that, too.

It was weary sophistication he quoted—
not an attempt to be original.

Laurie Duggan
hated that aspect of it—
which I think Queensland

'applies' to poetry.

Why he hated it—readings everywhere,
full of any pizzazz *but* poetry—

poetry being
'so unsaleable'.

I said, Yes, I'd go
out of gratitude—for finally being asked somewhere—

& have resented it ever since—well, resented it
for about a minute each week, lately.

Till now, when I'm
quite excited.

I think I'll wear a suit. I think
I may read well.

    (Laurie's experience
was they put him under a staircase somewhere
& left it off the program

& scheduled something else
as competition.) (I've never seen

Laurie in a suit. I've never heard him
not read well.
      We'll see.)

    The poems I've included,
do I apologise or simply offer warning?—

you're IN them—in a not-too
worrying way.

I'm reading now
some new Bolano—tell Stace. (Say 'hi' to her for me, of course.

I'll let her know what I think
as I read them:

if they're good or not.

How could they fail to be?
Did you read

The Savage Detectives, finally?

You didn't? I
loved it. I liked it from the start, began to tire, & then

the last
three-quarters got underway

(most of the book) & it was a
pure pleasure—

thoughtful & funny—

mostly sad—'realism', after all—but great—
with an amazing

farcical end.
I can't imagine these can beat it—

but maybe they will:

Nazi Literature of the Americas—
sounds good, doesn't it?

I forget the other title—but it has very long sentences, no
paragraphs
(a little testing to begin).

(Inform the girl!)

It will be a parade of crazies—
fictional, but true—

a gallery of weirdo authors
(extremists, bizarros, creeps, & people who

just
'misread the situation').

(I can see for some
the dream of national renewal—

but it's such a state of *rectitude,*
& *punishing demand*—as well as

uniformity & secrecy—the banishment
of all private life). Well, it appeals to some, obviously,

or it seems to them something else.

     Did you go to see
the Cy Twombly show?

some little scribbles, where I started
a recalcitrant biro, remind me to ask.

He's a troubling, anomalous figure
in my mind. I became aware of him,

initially,

in the 70s, struck by his name: ads in *Artforum*
showed his things

but articles in the magazine
never mentioned him. He was in European galleries.

He always seemed to me
Exquisite Good Taste. And I assumed

that was why the critical silence—
in the era of the reign of minimalism.

(Although, the reign continues.

And, *although* the reign continues,
his reputation has grown—

hard to do, for an
American in Europe.)

He was a friend & contemporary
of Johns & Rauschenberg

but chose to stay in Italy. Maybe
you know all this. The slow, slow rise to prominence.

He seems
an outer limit of Abstract Expressionism

—or some minimalist reduction of it,

to focus on process. "Pure mark making"
I once saw it described as

(to my delight).

It still sounds ridiculous to my mind.
"Give me Robert Ryman," I say

(& rest my case).

'Cy' comes from 'Cyclone', I read, a week or so ago—
a name his father took

after another 'Cyclone'
died or retired.

The family worked in circus.
So the name was appropriate—

to some sort of "feats of daring". What I find
so upsetting is that,

if he's famous now, then
I knew about him for 20 years

but didn't get the message.

Irrational, I know.

Plus
I still distrust the seductive quality of the paintings:

too much is being given, too easily—we are asked
too much to swoon.

Here I stand, probably,
with Rosalind Krauss—with whom I never stand, ordinarily.

I picture us
at a bus stop.

Have we both missed the bus?
No, Rosalind is waiting for a different one, a different bus entirely.

Taxi! my figure shouts. Anyway,
go & see the show

& report on it.
A recent English paper was gratifyingly ambivalent,

only half persuaded.

That
Picasso-Matisse show... was terrific

though too adversarial:

here we have Picasso
doing this, here we have Matisse. It suited Picasso,

who worked that way,
producing summaries of painting.

This is how it's done, here's a way
of doing *this* & so on.

Matisse worked more patiently—& had
a higher ratio of hits,

(was more of a colorist, was so often perfect,
surpassing). The contest

is exciting—but not the point.
Not Matisse's point certainly.

Maybe Picasso's, a match-point player.

I guess I'm agreeing—
Picasso wins—but protesting,

happier not making the choice,
I'd rather be looking at the paintings.

Though the mind *will* make comparisons.

Seeing people
from my past—I'm here with them, this week, in Brisbane—

makes me think of Sydney—where I knew them—
where I left aged thirty—& think then

of Michael Fitzjames—his paintings—
which I've been writing about lately. These are

city-scapes, done from
photos taken in the air, in the 30s or 40s (surveyors' photos).

The odd view, & the fact
that the buildings—many—have changed, defamiliarizes the city

but its basic outlines mean
we recognize it, gradually—

or recognize it immediately,
but can't say at first why it is strange.

I think, because I left Sydney—
never having been quite at home there—

& it is my parents' city,

Sydney seems for me
historical—

a city of particular artists—& struggles—& failures:
'Five Bells', Slessor, Grace Crowley,

Tony Tuckson,
Tony McGillick—

a city lost.

I feel detached from it sometimes—
at others a little defeated by it—

or, anyway—
objective about it, clear-eyed, so I can see

its self-image, its
unselfconsciousness,

its truths, evolutions, &
my own identifications. A city

lost to me. I doubt you feel this
about Adelaide

(which, admittedly. bears less of its history)

& you wouldn't feel defeated.
(You'll have terrific memories of London in later life—

& be able to go back to it.
You'll be—in fact you are already—

more of a man of the world,
more travelled, than me.)

        Michael currently has
a giant painting of Naples—

not the famous harbour,
a central part of the old town—

employing the same high point of view
as in the Sydney paintings—

a similar orange colour-scheme,

but, making it Italian,
small, isolated dabs of brighter colour—reds, greens

(window blinds? shop signs?),
like bits of glacé fruit in Italian ice cream.

I hear he's sold it.

    The Sydney pictures
are drier. They show the area

around Central Railway station—
the dental hospital, the park opposite, Grace Brothers

down from the Uni,
Broadway, Chippendale,

endless little roofs & windows,
& streets like canyons

cut in dried mud: a creamy brick-red
to ochre,

with the dark fissures
of the streets—in which shadow pools, black or dark blue.

Not many trees, seemingly,
back then. The trees in

Sydney's Hyde Park
are beautiful. They've grown a lot since I was a kid

& must have been
quite small & sparse—not grand at all—

when my father knew them:
now they suggest

mature, major metropolis—

like New York & Central Park,
or ... where else? I don't know.

But they should be painted
by Soutine, Chagall, Kirchner,

Wakelin, Frater, &
dated 1930.

I dream before them, or did
when I was last there,

of the innocence & wishes—& experience—

of my father's generation
(since they planned the thing,

their war memorial is in it,
etcetera).

My mother would have shopped there
as a girl—

Elizabeth St.,
Martin Place—or were

times then too tough?—

she'd have registered the glamour.
Though I think the glamour

has only recently arrived—a lifetime on the drawing boards,
'in development'. It was their city though

in a way that it was never mine.

It was smaller, more possessible.
And then the bridge crossed the harbour.

Hmm, Cy Twombly.

That's right. My old joke about him
was to put the words of bluff King George—

to Gibbon on the publication of *The Decline & Fall*—
in the mouth of someone

like Donald Brook

(austere, cool-ly cerebral, doubter
of most things 'aesthetic')

"Scribble, scribble, scribble—eh, Mr Twombly?"

a notion that always amused me.
"Pure mark making", beyond its

evident foolishness, has something to it—
but not very much. It indicates

the extreme, attenuated development
of the expressionist aesthetic. Actually, 'decline & fall'—

all those readings of the work
as palimpsest, as ravishing sensuousness, & regret for

lost civilization—

the Picturesque's 'love-of-ruin', of Time (time *passing*,
romantically—& 'cruelly'—& implacably, etcetera—

a delicious pathos). Wildness & refinement.
To me they seem an indicator

of something Roman & barbaric,

the West at the end of its tether.
But then, so many things can indicate that.

Ravishing surfaces, & high-minded,
or at least 'informed',

nostalgia—pathos savoured,
mementi mori & *lacrimmae rerum*—

& the alacrity of his line.

Maybe I am resisting too much.

Brisbane has been fun—well
organized—a lot of amateurish, not very serious writing,

of the kind
that is always around, new or withering,

but always a new generation.
The editor of one of the magazines actually the worst example.

(She even teaches the stuff.)

Some old friends are here: Steve Kelen,
Alan Jefferies, Helen & Peter—& Walt,

now looking teen-age & cool. Striking Petra White.

Some new names are very promising—
a young Russian woman, Veronika Tong, seems good,

& a few others. Some of
the organizers are of interest. The new 'wave', though,

looks awful:
highly skilled—

formal, 'poetic', indirect—well-mannered.
'Nice'—yet 'deep'—

satisfying someone's desire
for poetry as solace, as retreat from life,

as old-world wisdom,
buffed & burnished & mysterious.

As one prize-winner
was reading a sample of her stuff

Laurie's lines came back to me: "Poetry
was beginning to wear its formal jacket again

& speak in muted tones
of the edifying architecture of Venice."

Is that how it goes? Anyway, this was
everything we were against. But, then,

we lost that battle in our own time—
to the acolytes of Les—Jamie, Robert Gray, & others—

& the mystifications of Adders.
These were theirs.
                    Really,
I wouldn't have had such a good time—
if I'd lived there like Laurie.

It might all have seemed
predictably ramshackle—un-knowing—

&, on the other hand, *deliberate*—
pleased enough to casually slight

who or what did not fit,
unable to see the relevance.

But I was up to see it in the best light
& did.
           I'm back now. Pleased to be.

The *Nazi Literature* book is not the same hoot
or same pathos & ... humanity, the rest ... as *Savage Detectives*

but good. A few times I laughed out loud.

Your place in London sounds good.
Am I correct in imagining you at the top of a hill?

The very top?
Telegraph Hill.

One day you will see an old film—but which, & why?—
from RKO, & see the cartoon illustration—

a radio tower, small shed under it, a parked, forties car
(what, all this detail?), jagged bolts of electricity out in the sky

indicating broadcast:
how I picture you. I mean,

do you come out & think, *Which*
way will we walk down now? Is it all below you?

Or are you on one side (but high up, I gather)?
It's enough that it's in a part of London I don't know.

And part you don't either—or didn't.
But you say you are exploring still

& still enamoured of it—small Asian groceries
& shops,

where "Asia" doesn't mean simply (as
the UK now usually employs it) Indian, Pakistani,

but also Chinese, Vietnamese etc. Variety.

#

Brisbane is so un-Adelaide. As you'd expect:
rich, young, a little glossy & uncivilized & shallow.

The art galleries there
abound—but scream décor! design! buy me!

One of the artists was Wayne Eager, or some such.
Comical surname. They all had pictures,

one or two in storefront windows
—paintings or photos—

big, colourful & *brightly lit*—so you could
see the simple patterns

(*"bold* patterns", I stand corrected) & the authographic texture.
More focused than Cy Twombly—

less reference to Culture. Less reference
altogether. Just 'Art'. (Small 'a'.) A bit like

some of the poetry—

but higher production values
(cotton duck, good paint), & professionalism,

more akin to real-estate:
the bad poetry had *no* aura.
                                        These pictures at least said
"BrisVegas", or "Don't ask *Why*—feel the width!"

"Bold, isn't it?" the dealer must beam,
at the young couple about to purchase,

rising up & down on the balls of his feet,
hands behind his back, feeling like an idiot—

but soon to be that little bit richer!
The rent! The rent!

                        #

                        Yep, I'm back now.
Back a week: the EAF has had an opening,

I've finished Bolano (in bed this morning)
(I liked it—but it's not a serious attack on the right—

perhaps they don't deserve it.
It has that one last entry

that is chilling—
lifted from another book, verbatim),

& now I'm having coffee, writing this,
a hundred yards from Radio Adelaide—

where Cath will finish up, in a minute & join me.
(She'll run out

from under the tower,
jump in the pick-up truck … & drive on down.)

(I'll be played by William Bendix,
or Dan Duryea!)
                    (Cath might be …

Joanne Dru?)

It was good speaking on the phone this week.
See you in December!

I picture your view, out & down,
over a basin of roofs in late afternoon sun,

a silvering light, the skyline broken occasionally
by a dome or spire—peaceful but huge, an enormous

canvas for one's life. London.
                                    December!

                          Lots of love,
                          Ken

Contretemps

*for John Forbes, & friends — & Harry Mathews, and Jackie
Gleason, Audrie Meadows, Art Carney & the woman who played
'Trixie'*

On the very idea of a conceptual scheme
dogs start up a kind of barking.

"They built the basilica
on battered bones & bombed it."

And I can only say, as Hooker said before me—
"Boom Boom, Boom Boom,"

or as Fats Waller—curiously—before him:
"Boom boom boom—There's the curse back at you!"

"Stop that howling!"
A line I can't place—but apposite—I hear on a set,

like the one that housed Audrey
and 'Ralph Cramden' (Audrey, of course, was 'Alice')

& I remember the window they looked out of:
lovely, 'token'. Sometimes

Ralph would open it—on painted pipes,
a fire escape opposite, and a presumed alley—

& yell for Norton.
Did they ever yell

"Stop that howlin!"—
as I imagine?

Boom boom boom

(Would that they would—
there's those dogs—

sensing, plainly, a 'conceptual
scheme'—where, *I* think,

one is hardly apparent)
and a neighbour

—Norton?—
pounds loudly on the ceiling.

— Such a quiet pleasure, Poetry —

I turn on TV, the sound way down,
because of the neighbour—

and there's John Forbes, in black & white,
on the set of *The Honeymooners*. Just he—& their plain

kitchen table. I stare.
Momentarily he seems puzzled.

But goes to the window—& jumps out.
And is standing just outside

—the illusion of height it created:
I am amazed (!) —

and amazed
that I *am* amazed.

He has not 'fallen to his death'—
even a 'cartoon' death—& walks off.

In come Pam & Laurie,
followed by Cath & John—

Johnny J.

"Are you there, Ralphy boy?" asks Laurie.
I see them all 'listening'—for a reply.

I wonder does Forbes
say anything, in this dream?

I adjust the volume:
and hear what they hear—Garbage bins

being knocked about, dogs barking.)

Exotic Things

(from a travel journal)

(TUNIS—IN THE GREEK RESTAURANT)

in the Greek restaurant we ordered dilemmas.
I had one with lemon.

(ENIGMA)

in Africa we shot enigma (which, in Africa,
only foreigners trouble to call "enigma",
everyone else, quite unselfconsciously, calls them
"enigmas").

(PRONE)

on the lakes, near the coast, fed by the massive
Victoria Falls further inland, we saw the graceful
long-legged *prones;* & then, more difficult to see
but quite easy to catch, & calm once you held them
in your hands, the smaller supine. They provide
the imagery for much of the poetry in those languages
for their soft sad eyes & the softness of their
feathers. Tourists, on the other hand, only know
the prone, whose silhouette, in postcards, especially
against the lake at dawn or dusk, is readily available.

(PASSION FRUIT)

It is April.
We drove across Sudetanland in Robert's
Irrational—something like the bigger
Wilys utility panel-van of the late 50s
but made in Africa by a Dutch firm, &,
curiously, with the 'British' name—the
four of us & Robert, who drove, & an
American who was a photographer, who wasn't
going very far.
                        We left the American &
Robert at the coast & bought a car (an old
Renault) & made good time, & in reasonable
comfort, though we felt a little cramped
after the Irrational.

At the border we saw passion fruit.

(BIROS)

six months later, as we recrossed the border, there were
biros. Everywhere! eating the passionfruit (that had,
meanwhile, ripened). They even hung from the vines, &
further on they were all along the cane-&-rope
bridge, that hung above the ravine, & refused even
to budge—as we made our way across. In fact, *as*
we crossed, as the bridge swung with our weight, their
chirruping became even louder & more insistent & filled
the whole valley, whose trees, beneath us, were full of
them, invisibly. The sound was as of an aviary.
They are bigger than, but very like, finches, & are called
by the natives *bic bic*. On the bridge, they were perched
along the handrails, almost 'shoulder to shoulder', & would
not move as we crossed.

(A STRANGELY EXOTIC LIFE)

It was funny, that one of the most exotic things
was in the little village, near the border, where
Robert & the Irrational were to meet us & pick us up;
& where we stayed fully four days, as he had had
trouble with the truck (the roads were bad after the
summer rains)… funny, that one of the most exotic
sights was that of a *Life* magazine in the village.
A single copy. It was offered to us & we all read
it.

('A GIFT')

We loaded the supplies—all that Robert & his
wife would need for most of the next six months—
into the truck, & enjoyed the trip, inland this time,
as Robert drove us back. This trip had been for us
an excuse to see more of the country, but at
Mfuwa, aside from getting Robert's supplies & some
parts he had ordered for the truck, we booked our
airline tickets. (A charter truck would take us,
next time, to the coast.) For Robert & Joan we got
an extra case of white wine. It was Portuguese,
inexpensive, & very good. A gift.

(DILEMMAS AGAIN)

in the little Greek restaurant, back at the coast,
where we'd sat that morning, we sat again, waiting out
the time to our flight, we again ordered dilemmas.
Thus rounding our journey off—as it was Robert,
in a letter, who had first told us of the restaurant
& how to find it.
            That first time we had been
wondering what our hosts would be like. & now,
leaving, we of course thought of them.

(A STRANGE LIFE)

When we returned, before I got—seriously—back
to work, I visited Tony in his studio, near where Jill
& I live (& where I myself had once worked—I'd given
the studio up, for the trip, rather than pay rent). I
tell you this because it was only a week after I'd got
back, & it reminded me of Africa—Tony had somehow
got hold of a grisaille. He had it in his studio, tied
to a perch by a very fine chain. It was only small but
expressive & carefree—in a quiet, subdued sort of way.

It was funny to arrive home & find this little piece of
Exotica, even here, in Paris.

An artist friend of Tony's, he said, had one in New York.

"A Few Days

Are all we have. So count them as they pass.
    They pass too quickly,"
says Jimmy Schuyler.
                     Today began not so well,
but at first I think of Anna tonight humming at
    ten years of age
a Sonny Boy Williamson song—that she has
    picked up from me—<u>I'm so proud</u> '!' Well, 'amused'—
I hum it too & we dance for a bit. Earlier,
    Cath, Anna & I go out for coffee—something
sweet—& meet, fortuitously, George & Carlo—
    George (Georgina) with her second son
at the coffee shop of tout
    le monde—'tout',
anyway, of this part of the world. Not like
    Rundle Street, where the action
really is. King William Road—Hyde Park—is for the
    stiffer gentry—&,
for their rich children, a near-enough-to-home
    amenity. Well, it
does for us. Before that Anna & Cath played
    flute together.
Thinking back, I realize,
    the day started with a ride into town, the paper,
then the attempt to use the bromide machine, whose
    complexities, now, no one understands—
& nor did I. Old technology. A skill
    I had once, forgotten..
After that I came home, showered, calmed down
    & set to some final odds & ends—
a date with the printers, some time—
    in
the next few weeks—details of design: that I love.
    I worry: the imagery is

too American—tho it's not exclusively—& I
        shuffle images around.
As I work I listen to Crab's band,
        The Cocktail Hour they were called—or
more precisely *Crab's Cocktail Hour* circa 1985
        with its endless, demented patter between *every*
song, that reaches high points of cynicism,
        frankness, disinterested bile, disinterested
curiosity even—& surprised-by-joy discovery, where
        Crab & Arnold say things that surprise even them
& are amused. As well, the band are at cross purposes
        never has the word "shutup" been so much used. It
'all works out for the best' in a terrific finale
        where Crab makes a speech that parodies
an impromptu MC at a bingo party thanking
        all for coming & putting
the 'best face on things'. Nights at Lark & Tina's
        really were—to quote one of the band's
chosen preoccupations for the night—
        A Long Day's Journey Into Night.
Really a long night working to dawn—rapport
        between band & audience
(like the love between Liz & Richard
        in *Virginia Woolf*) acknowledged finally with the
last two songs & the encore.
        We knew
we'd lived another day &, en route, had seen some Real Life.
Nightclubs made me uncomfortable—they still do—
        I'm was lucky to be introduced
by Mary & Micky & Crab
        to that particular scene. My friends in
Sydney & Melbourne never saw it. And it was only that
        one club, that one band. (*Speedboat*
was musically superior, yes, but was much less about values.
        Or they were more purely musically expressed?—
with the same personnel, the *Cocktail Hour* was a tour of duty,

the whole experience.) Anyway, I experience them again,
two or three times over, in the afternoon, in my room, down the
back,
gluing this, drawing that, looking
for useable images, noting corrections. This magazine
will be ready. Cath comes home
with the Banana, who watches television, demands food,
borrows a pencil for her homework, while Cath sits
reading on the lounge near her, calm. Dinner, &
then the flute thing. The night is nearly over
because we've managed all on the same night for a change
to be tired together
& hit the bed early—tho Gabe comes in, lateish,
from the other house (his father's).
But goes to bed, quickly. Only I
am up late, scribbling. A letter to Pam
to write, maybe, a letter to another poet. James
Schuyler to read. Crab to ring—to-
morrow.
Mary I should ring or see more often. And
Dave, whose daughter died. I wrote—late enough—
to say I'd visit, & haven't still.
I live on the other side of what is only a very small city.
Large enough to come between us.
I am going to ease myself
into my usual state of anxiety.
Ah, equilibrium, you have found me! Mildly
Crazed, mildly happy—happier, really, than that.
I turn off the light.

Poem ("I do a drawing ...")

       I do
a drawing, from
a photograph

of Jimmy Rushing
arriving in New York
—or Chicago :

maybe that is
the 'El', going
overhead.

He looks great
in the photo
and okay in the drawing

so I spray the drawing
with fixative,
& think about

going into
town —
for a drink

this thing
completed
making me

suddenly feel good,

as good as Jimmy
looks to feel
in the photograph.

I put my watch on
& take it off
(thongs too)

& sit again at
the desk, where a
clipping George sent says:

Otis Rush
backed by * the Hounds
* live * at the Village Gate *

beside a small picture
of Otis looking
pretty heavy,

& pretty classy,
& dude-ish too.   A
high-contrast

'tone dropout'
it stands
against a small dish

with paperclips
& buttons in it
& a tiny artificial

flower—
cream-yellow petals—
from Hazel's dress.

There, too,
beside a patch of
bright red on something

is a large badge
that belonged to my paternal
grandfather

it's cream,
with a little shot
of him

on it —
his ID,
for his job

minding American ships
during WW II

a night-watchman
he stares back balefully,
looks like me,

though a tougher guy.
He hated yanks.

Yanks were who
he was tough to.
Though I

heard a story
about diving
into the water

to save a
Swede he'd
punched out.

Tucker Bolton.
I guess he'd lost

some weight
by the time this photo

was taken—
the only one
I have of him.

He died soon after
—in the war —
a heart attack

getting up one night
to go & mind
the wharves

I never met him.

He looks like me
on my last
book of poems.

Between him &
me stands my father.
I feel my features

merge back through his,
my father's,
to those of the man

on this badge—
a mug shot,
head & shoulders—he stands

in front of a grid
of heights,
and is my height,

I can see, a shade
under the line that indicates
5 feet 9.

His name is a line under him
Thomas B Bolton
& under this

April 14, 1943, B.

around the photo
lots of USA initials, the
words Civilian Personnel,

& his number
B 2431.

I am Ken Bolton
& live in Adelaide

a poet, heir
to the toughest man
in Double Bay & Edgecliff, back then,

the father of my father.
Both of us violent.

In a way
that never gets expressed—
even through violence.

I look at the
tiny photograph.

Luminous Hum

Maybe
        After all these years it turns out
I'm some sort of 'Art Brut' type

              — in fact an outsider
                     artist

Peculiarly focused on the idea
            Of being cool

my idea of which (naively)
            is the New York School
                #
                      (joke?
          #
"on me")

        why —tho I have the fee—
           they'd never have me
I'd of course pay Ted
        I took them 'seriously' (?)
             or 'too' seriously ?
The art world
      — I tell Grogan

          whoever —

     gives the art world too much credit
it wasn't Anton's gig

(You don't know him, Ross?
         six four
weighs about 70 k
       Blond

As *I* am blond

blonder!

rather Eton—
Oxford—
Wilfred Owen)

The bass players ...
they do that thing
seen
in the credits, once, every week
in the *Gomer Pyle* show
of playing catch-up — the
quick
½ step brings you back with the others
left right

Flying High
(was a movie)
(I know)
'Flying Home' might have been *the* jazz standard —
of around 1950,
1940?
not so much a standard
who plays it now?
but a kind of hit
&
fodder for bands to process
tho
... I think I like it,
I think

No idea of it now   ·

                                        two second-order bands
                                                of that era
                                                play it

                                        (on a CD I have)

on a joint gig
                        something they could *agree to do*
                                                together

I'm flying on,
                — maintaining altitude—

on 4 or 5 short blacks & as many retsina chasers
                                #
the jazz, then, is some Coltrane—Coltrane 'live' in Europe,
courtesy of Crab—
                                right at the moment
                                                playing
(not Crab — Coltrane
                        tho Crab could 'as easily'
be playing it
                        strange thought
                                                in the suburbs
                                                on his saxophone
                                                in Dulwich

                                                'Bye-
Bye Blackbird'
                tamer
                than the
                'Village Vanguard'
                or
                'wherever' version
                I have &
                usually play.

: "Live

in Europe"

it occurs to me, is a very

North American

locution,

like "It was raining in America"

was European

— (Which

journalist tried that?

My sympathy, pal)—

An

American locution itself ("Pal").

#

'Live'.

#

Where in Europe — Spain?

the Netherlands?

Paris?

Anyway, the

bass is very comforting

The thing I love about

the Bye-Bye gig

—"his greatest concert performance"

is the subtitle : I can't find

the booklet

where it says, probably, 'where' it is

—Vanguard,

5 Spot (did he record there, ever?

too early, too late, too hostile, too...)

Birdland?—

it's surely in summer, a fairly hot night (?)

euphoric is the word I always want to reach for
the sense of release, potted palms, the urge to drink
take drugs, breathe in know that you're alive
& others, other constituents—the moon, probably,
somewhere visible

     offering

       encouragement

Granpa Simpson

    —a novelty, benign, 'Granpa Simpson' *cork*—

is stuck in my bottle

      keeping the last glass of

        retsina

fresh

    #

   Must get ice.

      (Gets ice.)

       #

       The band

is now Chasin the Trane

      Coltrane

       sounding

both 'elixir-happy' & 'effortful' & THE DRUMMING
      IS FANTASTIC : Elvin

      Elvin!

    it is great the way art
    hands this sort of thing
   on

     #

    even poetry

     #

      For more

       people,

                                        tho,
music must do it.

I'm with them.
                    You people,

                                    don't be so
                                    stand-offish

I'm clearly drunk?
                Clearly ?
                            Drink up then.

Tho it isn't so—I'm not
                    Tho *the spirit*
                                — the spir*its* —

                                    of the great dead
watch over me
                & laugh
                            or nod
                                    (they're
not entirely against)
                    : Philip Whalen,
                                        Ted,
Larkin
            YIKE!
                    Dame Edith Sitwell

                                — Go To Bed (!)

John Forbes

John, how funny how appropriate how
                                    ironic
but in any case John! how are you

it's *your line*

of course

you saluted "their luminous hum"

I don't believe there

Is anything

after death

Which doesn't preclude, I guess,

that there should be

This urge

a sort of Willed Short Circuit

where the present winds the past forward

to talk to it

\#

solace

\#

"if you insist on doing that you'll tangle the

hose

& have to come back to it iron out the kinks"

—an image this from my watering.

John,

You were so un-suburban (as I imagine you)

You were never very thoughtless.

Can I see you standing, holding a hose?

Thoughtless thought.

Maybe you did.

Is it such a joy?   your 'speed'??   Speed *was*

was more your speed.   Ha ha.

But I don't say that

laughing at you : you did what you did & I liked

you.

Do the dead "hum", "luminously"?

Last week

they celebrated the anniversary of your death
commemorated the death /

           celebrated the poems, *you.*
     Predictable?

               A good
turnout—
     the young were there in force, the old
(people your age if you'd hung on

John Forbes at 58

         No doubt you'd have carried it
off)
   all there.

        Some Japanese people down the front ...
               'curiously'.
     —the kind of "curious" you'd have
           applauded
        as a detail—
a further guarantee of your future
       you who have none
         who
don't exist.
     I cling on
       — & remember you —
tenaciously
     —what, "cling"? "remember"?
            cling:
I remember okay
     In fact I don't even 'cling'
       tenaciously (" ")

but swing & sway here   from my branch,
        a
happy sloth

while Charlie Parker, Coltrane,
Art Pepper, Art
Blakey

Pepper Adams

play

Tho it could just as easily be

? & the Mysterions

remember them, or
Thane
Russall

'& Three'

Voom-voom voom-voom, voom-voom voom-vcoom
Voom

"I want s-e-c-u-r-i-t-y!"

ha ha

It is

permitted

to laugh?

Pal?

(a thread I forgot)

Finally
I recognise this track — it is "My Old Flame"

The album

—(I think Crabby made this tape

thank you, Crab

— my pal —

my *old* pal) —

it's not listed on the cover, it just says

#

Not one I know

#

I know enough to put
ice in this glass—

Phil, Ted?

Edith!

"go to bed"

which I take to be their luminous numinous
humorous hum

Schuyler,

Frank,

Joe … are up there too, an
unlikely scenario

Auden, I suppose
would give me
some kind of talking to

#

I'll go I think & find my sandals   hose the
bamboo quietly

go to bed

#

Cath's away —

Anna & Chris down the back.

Pola / has disappeared
to be with them & share the air-conditioner.

Will

jazz make me cool?

          Phil ??

will Joey Ramone?

The 'Conception' stuff sounds straighter.

Tho was Coltarne ever straight?

                  That was

Miles' problem

        — 'with' him —

                  & Miles'

problem later

this track too sounds like 'My Old Flame'
transposed

        weirded

            made strange

strangely freighted

           with a more abstract

foreboding

        or a withholding of trust

it has none of the original's reassurance
more the recollection of the old flame's
            unreliability

        #

shit, how 'mature'

        at this hour of the night

        #

                              will
my spirits recover

                    John, my guardian angel,
what a funny idea
                    who would Wim Wenders get
to play you?   You'd say "Yeah, he'll recover" —
                    referring to me —
speaking from experience

                         #

                    I tend to see everyone
as more serious than me
                         tho they can't all be —
or I'd take them more seriously

                         #

                         "See, that's
what I mean!" you say   to Ted, Whalen, Joe —
"he'll be okay."

                    John, thank you.

                              Grace to be awake
& stay awake
              as long as possible!

Will I sleep the sleep of the dead, now, luminously?

              Grace to be awake

         That will be my endeavour
         & tomorrow "Ring Crab"!

Mary, Mill

Dear Mary & Dear Mill,

I've been meaning to write

for months now.

(Not sure what there is to report—

but I'll *FIND OUT*.)

'Meaning to write.'

I know you know the feeling—

because *everyone you know*'s

on the other side of the world:

(so)   you owe

Half The Planet a letter!

Something

you'll have come to terms with by now.

I'm sitting in our beautiful back room

— Easter Monday —

which is chiefly yellow in feel

(the room, that is —

&, 'hence', the day?)

Probably

a little too much yellow

but it's a comforting colour.

The yellow is a milky,

orange,   bread-crust colour—

the dappled light

hitting the pencil blinds

that Cath found

for all the windows.

So,

where the room looked

       Australia's idea of

          'slightly Japanese',

with its former paper blinds,

       it now looks (one Australian's idea of)

African—except

       the scene out the blinds

          & out the open door

is the russet Provencale

       of grape-vine leaves

          &, beyond,

the usual 'Yalta-conference-look'

       scattered deck chairs—

          & folding chairs—

& cane chairs—that Cath invariably

       has in the yard

          —

       minus

       Stalin, Roosevelt & Churchill.

Which is good.

       I'd hate running backwards & forwards

taking *them* cups of tea.

       To the left is

          the trampoline,

that I can't envision either of the three using,

       though it's fun to try.

       I liked the photo you sent—

       of a bonboniera shop—

          in Barcelona?

Buenos Aires?

       Mexico?

       I'll find it & check.

It reminded me

        of my late 80s view

              of *Al Frescos*

from the Rundle Street Writers' Centre—

              though more authentically

Euro

      or Latin

         in feel.

             Having travelled

                  and seen those things

I'm less nostalgic for them now.

            "Nostalgic" can't be right?

                   No

—but the local instance

            might stimulate

                a longing for the originals?—

   'known' only in the way

the amputee's phantom limb is imaginable:

             your left arm

          (Rundle Street)

reminding of the missing right

      (Seville, where you've never been).

I still drink at *The Flash* every second morning

               (apropos the

above)

I couldn't 'go'

      to the place across the road,

           where the former *Flash* used to be,

without a sense of betrayal. Not

        —gulp!—

             that I haven't

betrayed
        people in my life.

            It is the better spot—
                  the original *Flash*'s.

So, here, it's just me,
        and the old Italians,
                and the workaholics—i.e.,
not the Italians,
        but me & the
              rest, industriously reading papers,
marking essays,
        dreaming up 'the poems'
                — while the social set
sit across the road chortling
        and slapping backs.
                It has worked out
okay
      —in terms of productivity
             (except
             the *Flash* now
charges
      twenty cents more than anybody else,
             for an
unpredictable coffee).

      A night out with Crabby looms
      in the coming week or so.
      Can I face it?
        They require stamina.

                I spent a while this morning
                  trying to figure
the cover of my next book.

I'm pretty drawn to another version
of Boofhead.
Simple visage,
simple design, too.
Or even
a single Malamatina bottle top,
featuring the little tippling man
with the key in his stomach—
though that would indicate
a greater devotion to retsina—

&

by extension to alcohol—
than is the truth.

Otherwise,
I have:
) a still-life,
) a drawing of me,
) a photo of Lee Marvin.

I should send you copies—
a fistfull of Adelaide sensibility, arriving
in your tiny Tokyo flat.

Alongside
yours & Mill's.
(Sensibilities
that must be, still,
slightly Adelaide
but in need of reinforcement?)

'Millswood' —
how I used to like to think of you.
By

analogy
with *Kingswood Country* —

where the expectations—& vision—of

Ted Bullpit,

    or whatever his name was,

        ruled.

        Millswood country, Mill,

would be a place that ran

    on your loveably nutty principles.

          My

idea of them

    was your running to the car in the mornings

        for your lift to school, dropping

homework & carrying your shoes

    while Mary called for you to hurry.

You seemed wonderfully, amusingly,

    innocent & carefree & charmed.

    I'm sure

Millswood Country runs

    on more rational principles now.

        But the

matinee

of your teenage years

    was great to witness.

        Please forgive

this take on you.

    (I'm sure you've always seen *me*

        —much more accurately—

as a cross between

    Eeyore   & Bullwinkle. True?)

        I have

a large picture of you

    from two or three years ago

        Michael gave me.

I keep it

      in my Frank O'Hara *Collected*

            so I see you every month or two:

looking beautiful,

      judicious,

         ("feminine, marvellous & tough"—

in Ted Berrigan's phrase).

            The expression

(in the photo)

      very like Mary's in similar moods—

           probably the same mood.

    It looks like *you*

        —or she—

           are trying to look into the

             future.

Or maybe you're about

      to utter the phrase,

         "Smoke-signals"

           —and,

sure enough, small puffs

      rise from the distant hills,   drums.

        #

      Those restless natives!

        #

        I hope you're having

        a good time there, Mill.

     Are you & Mary spending

a lot of it together?

    Hey, your friend Charity — I remember

          you & other girls

all sniggering & snuffling with laughter

      at a barbequeue once

        at Westbury Street

when I called her Chastity

— by (far too
accurate?) mistake.

I think she was having
'boy-friend trouble' ...

It's been nice working with her
upstairs at ANAT
these last few years.
Tho the organization
has just moved—near
the *Flash*
in Hindley Street.
So I don't see her so often.
Charity's had a bad time
lately:
some creep broke in to
her house & robbed it
while she was locked
in her bedroom & freaking out.

A bit shakey these last
few weeks, I gather.

Mary, I've been in touch
with Martin recently.
He's in Hong Kong,
—a little 'out of town',
from the mainland—
where
Bernie is teaching English.
He has managed to persuade the Australia Council
he can
'work from home'
—he handles out-of-
Australia projects anyway.

His commuting time has been

                    cut "to seconds", he says—

                                    as he trips

from bedroom to kitchen

              & laptop.

                    Jyanni—you might

have known already—

        is teaching in (I think Northern?) China.

I can give you

          contact details

                  if you like. Though

would this only aggravate

              'the correspondence problem'?

Bessie Smith is on

      — 1923 —

          "Aggravatin' Papa".

        Hence the word "aggravate".

                      I think

because you told me

        about getting lost in the snow

                  trying to find your

                        way

back to your door

        —early days for you in Tokyo—

                  whenever

I picture you guys

        it is in the snow:

              #

              you both have hoods on

consequently

      that give, *consequently,*

Snugglepot-&-Cuddlepie

frames

     to your faces

          & make your eyes very big & beautiful.

Funny?

    Nuts?

       (Not so?!)

          I never think

          of almond or

          peach blossom

          blowing about

—but it's Spring there soon,

       right?

         So the snow

will have melted,

     —off all the brutalist concrete—

             & somewhere

there must be some green.

    I'll send you some poems with this.

             One of them

talks about the O'Hara poem

      "The Day Lady Died";

          there's one for Simryn;

                    &

a long, nutty one   'about'

      Europe.

         (As well as deliberately

under-achieving—

     as a summative statement

     'on Europe'—

          it has some

ridiculously recherché

     High-Cultural references

         (Winckelmann,

is the one I remember.

                No one knows who

                he is these days, nor

                              should they, really—

the theoretician

            of early

                     neoclassicism.)

And another thing I've written,

                "The Circus".

                              Anyway,

it's about finished.

                I've left it for a few months

                          so I can read it afresh

& maybe notice the bits

                that need fixing—

                            differently than you do

when you're close to it.

                        But *The Circus* is what I'd

like to send you.

            You might both like it. I'll send it eventually.

That's it. There's more to say—

                and while I'll forget to say it

when I see you next

            I better leave it till then

                      & get *this*

packaged up—& in the mail.

            Hope you're keeping well.

I'll see Michael at an opening soon

            & he can tell me you're fine.

Hope you like the pix & poems.

(It's now
late in the afternoon. Outside,
wildebeest & roebuck,
hyenas,
even a few giraffe,
can be seen ambling past,
silhouetted
against the last of the sun.
Africa.
A pencil on the table near me
—about four inches long—
is casting a rectangle of shadow
that is about four inches by seven
(the sun is so low),
& a small bottle beside it is casting
an enormously long
tube of shadow.
It looks like avant-garde
1920s photography —
or advertising,
… of the sort that Cassandre,
the man who designed
the Malamatina label,
might have done.

What a small world I live in!

Unlike you.

Though I suppose
(it being Japan)
you each live in
very small rooms.

116

Stick up that picture of Boofhead
—& think of me!

Love, Ken.

(Monday) Hullo, Pam

"and the arts shall march in the very van" — Saint-Simon

Skinny poem today?—why not,
    tho there's nothing in the tank,
bar some

    abstract 'energy'.
I am reading tonight
    with the enemy—

well,
    the heartless competition
& must read well, give

no quarter,
    seem to exist
among other criteria exactly.

    But, Pam, dull palookas, mostly—
no trouble. But
    now, I must 'get to work':

an essay for some artists
    describing their show—its necessity,
beauty & weirdness

    absolute surprise, etcetera.
They like the draft so far
    —they would—

& I do like the show
    so I haven't had
to dissimulate too painfully.

Sarah's stuff I know &
Matt's—really
I know them all

Except Scott.
How long
have I been

missing him—or seeing
only what is atypical
so it slips from the memory?

And Christian Lock:
I've stared at a few,
very hard—

& liked them
& liked the problematic
they seem to live with,

carelessly. What-me-worry! Carelessness, in-
souciance,
their quality. Four

hundred dollars—
which I will take to *DJ*'s, buy new shoes.
Shod another year. (Five,

if I get them mended on schedule.)

A firm basis on which
to march
"in the very van"

ha ha
& write the skinny poem, for Pam

(ha ha) it wouldn't be about
    art reviews

—not that she's against them—
    art *or* art reviews—
but that I never talk about them

    with her concentration—
nor
    (even more to the point)

as if they're part of real life.
    The occasion
of writing is. The

    experience
of the art is. So why?
    I'm moving further away from it

like it less often—
    realize
it's not my game, my irrelevance *to* it

    something like that,
or like *those things*—
    tho this is to stab at the problem,

without much care for accuracy.
    Some I care about a lot:
I never required

    that I should count to the artists
(he said nobly)
    Nice, tho, when you did.

But I write it less—with less
mission. I like the stuff less often, too.
My ideas were out of fashion

Ten years before I found them
& then I developed them, a little,
with others equally unfashionable

which made for a kind of rigour,
or the 'feeling' of it—& a fall-back position
of a more forgiving, but

less approving, accommodation: good
cop, bad cop. Tho I think I avoided
the critic as Police.

The artists began to seem less serious—or
the art 'world'.
Some of the artists were, of course—

(serious)

& 'were', on levels I wasn't
relaxed about, or attuned to, but came to see, finally.
So, no art criticism. For you, Pam.

The everyday then? Monday
is our most everyday day
one we both have off. So Cath & I

shop, walk the dog, have lunch together
we boiled some artichokes for lunch—something
we first did in Rome. Pietro told us how.

We caught the bus
    to the Pasadena *Coles* (or *Big W?*)
Did he actually say "You boil the shit out of them"?

He may have, his English was quite Australian.

    As a young music student in Rome
he was befriended by an Australian composer.
    Meale? The owner of the only Schoenberg records

in the city
    & something of an inspiration, or model, for Pietro—
a model for bravery & isolation maybe—

fortitude, anyway, that Pietro evinced
    as a more or less black-balled practitioner—
after a university student-occupation.

    We took our shopping trolleys—the two-wheel
sort (one folds up & can
    go in the other).

    Then we caught the bus home again.

I walked the dog earlier,
    while Cath slept—as
she hadn't, properly, the night before.

    I read at intervals Bolano's book
The Savage Detectives—which I like: it's
    So shaggy-dog as a principle

yet, 'in principle', so much more serious
    or solemn, a solemnity
it pokes fun at—the solemn dignity

of Latin American Literature
the nobility, idealism, corruption, futility
ineffable sweetness etc etc

of its imaginary. (A word
that should be capitalized—but I can't bear
that 'Theory' should enter in, be

allowed in, here.

Tho in principle
(what a principled poem!), you know, like
Let the discourses mingle...

Let the flowers bloom, etcetera

I sort of don't like a word with a limited life
to crawl in, ... presuming, I guess,
my poem will outlive it. Fat chance? May be.

The other days are 'everyday'—in the sense
that they are unvarying—
but have less individuality about them:

I ride to work, have time to think & read or write,
a bit,
before work. Then I work—& ride home.

Things happen. Sure. And I have the odd idea—
or plenty of ideas—
because people think

& at work I'm alone most of the day, so my head
is where I'm at.
The same head every day. Monday

I get off that loop. I chopped wood a bit
today, which was fun &
         Moved washing around

In an attempt to get it dry. A CIA man says
         on TV
the war in Iraq is lost. Has

         been lost for some time
was never going to be won with so few troops deployed
         etcetera. Which the world has known

for a few years now. When did
         the CIA find out, I wonder? A free & frank
disclosure from the CIA—or even Bush—

what a funny idea! I don't want to talk this crap, either
         —here—
or use the word "crap" much, if it comes to that.

         Ah, *The Purity Of Diction*

         In English Verse—is that where I'm headed?
The day was clear, 'beautiful' (in
         inverted commas, but really, too)

We were happy. Cath swam, the dog barked
         (asked me to play with it, & I did—
she ran & hid for a second, then remembered

         she liked to be chased & came out)
& I chased her, cut the wood, read
         Bolaño. You?

ODD QUARTET

(BEGINNING WITH A POEM IN RON PADGETT'S MANNER, A NOCTURNE, WITH A NOTE FROM TED BERRIGAN)

Nocturne

for Pam Brown

Something makes me remember I've got an old *'C'* magazine—

I don't know where it is

& I'm not going to look for it right now—
(*"If you knew my room ..."* etcetera.)

What made me think of it? A glimpse
of *'Z'*, of which I have a full set

And I *picture* it

(big, a bit torn, soft paper going brittle)
then I thought of its name —

The 'C' / 'Z' connection —

Z magazine
C magazine.

That,
& the idea of writing something like Ron Padgett:

he mentions
a tiny statue,

of his friend
Tony Towle

with gloves
& an umbrella in its hands.

I've met Tony Towle.
He's pictured on my wall,

beside a drawing of Laurie Duggan,
& a 'latin' man —

drawn, the latter, as if the artist who drew *Boofhead* attempted
Willy De Ville. (The Tony Towle

and Laurie Duggan drawings on the other hand
are straightforward.) In

the magazine
is a letter from Ted,

handwritten—
not to me. It says

To give it back some time
it's his only copy.

Signed Ted

His big curvy signature—
lower case I think.

I picked it up
thirty years ago

as a curiosity—the gang's all there,
in it

& the note—

written late at night, I figure
(like now)

(Did Ted
'do' mornings?)

I always see it under a fluoro glare
I think I always imagine it

written in the kitchen

(piles of books around
& paper I suppose

but maybe that's because
I read it at night, every five or six years

                    … with paper,
piles of books around).

I should write a letter to Pam—

she quoted Ron
yesterday.

I was thinking
of writing to the list—

about their recommendations to Cassie
(read Rilke, read Milton, read so & so)

& saying,
as a joke,

"I believe these suggestions
are quite wrong—

she should be on a diet
of pure Padgett & Schuyler."

A joke—
that is something like my 'real' position.

My real position:
"Ron Padgett—great poet!"

There's

There's not much time. This
is probably not a poetry day.

Ron Padgett's
'What the desk said'

is the last thing on my mind.
That is,

the last thing I've read—
but not right now

the sort of thing
I want to write. Young guy,

in black tights
& black-with-

blue-stripe
top,

black beanie
blue on top, comes in:

like the sort of figure—
usually a girl—they use in AGL ads

(Australian Gas Light Company)

a bike rider of some sort.
My black biro runs out

—greys—
I panic

find one in my bag

& now I write in blue.
Over the road, the Weimar Room.

A page back, my
'notes' on Weimar

(the phrase
"the glue of human stupidity"

noted
down)

my notes
—a page or so before—

on liberalism (notes
for one of Anna's essays)

Liberalism
& its failures

Andy P is appearing
at the Weimar Room

me—I *dis*appear
from the coffee shop

to reappear—where?—
at work

where I'll lock into words again
a little like the beaver

that swims down river
beneath the ice, & surfaces

at the next hole

& resumes his life: *two
parallel lives*—one

of movement—& consciousness
& the eye's attention—

the other a dream of consciousness.
That's me,

I'm like that. The
beaver may see things differently

The Beaver's Poem

As I swim downstream I notice small fish swim by—
They give me a wide berth—

& bits of twig & grass—but otherwise the water is quite clear

& the light comes through the ice
More evenly than in summer & of course not as blue

A kind of moonstone, with the shadow, occasionally,
Of something fallen on it—a

Branch, a small patch of snow & leaves & dirt
But no cloud, no intense blue no flying birds—

Tho a bird sometimes walks there.
If I test the ice to see if it will break

They fly away
So I never do.

I push on,
Paddling pretty evenly, & I think about the hole

Up ahead, where I'll come out—& breathe again.
As soon as I picture it

I picture inevitably the things I'll see there:

About this time the cyclist goes by
On the road by the river—in his black & his blue in winter

(In summer he wears more variously coloured jeans
& shirt)

He studies at the University
I think—tho I have

Forgotten how I knew—
I wonder what he is studying—politics, military history—

Or something useful like medicine

I doubt he studies philosophy, the arts,
Art history, say: he rides too fast

You expect the poetic to ride slowly. Tho now I think about it
It's those *non*-disciplines, where ideas come easily,

Not crabbed & doubtful, where you *really* get to pedalling

Take me for example
I have practical things to do—I'm pretty much by definition a
              worker—

I paddle steadily.

In summer, when the ice is melted long away
& the skies are blue & fish are plentiful

Etcetera etcetera—un-troubled—
You'll find me sometimes shooting swiftly thru the stream

And I don't know *what* I'm thinking—if you asked me,
If you *were* to ask. But my mind is racing.

& that is how I see the typical poet
(Ron Padgett, maybe—

Cath Kenneally, Cassie Lewis—

Not Rilke
Maybe Heine!)

I think holding a pen must be just enough
To slow things down

Otherwise, they'll be lost in dreams.
I know mine are—*I'll never*

Have these thoughts again
Here we are. Breathe deeply.

The Mother's Poem

I ride this same ride every day & so it never seems
To get harder. Well, some days—

& then the day after it is easy again—*so*, basically,
Much the same. I think if I lived a life

Of relative adventure—rode each week to shop
In a different village—it would be much harder

I'd wear myself out—& feel my age, or older—the continual
Impact,

Of each scene & change of light & circumstance,
Registering, the mind taking it in: hardly time

To think about the usual things.

Riding here each day by the same river,
The scene pleasant, & reassuring in its dependable nature

My thoughts can dwell on what most matters

& not my riding.
& I never notice

How my riding goes—is it faster or slower
Is it slower & slower gradually—so gradually

That I can't notice? (I've thought about it here
But not at the conscious level—on which

It could sink in. I could have this thought again & never notice—
& will.

I think about the things I mean to think about

A daughter whom I love & her needs & cares—
Which at nineteen are hardly troublesome

In
Fact they are a kind of sunny triumph

A well-ordered life I like to share
& make run more smoothly: there will be troubles up ahead

This is where I almost always purse my lips
& pedal grimly the flat part where the road

Turns away from the river & where it joins the wider road
& there's the bus-stop. I think

That is why my mood always sharpens, just here,
I become conscious of myself as spectacle, on this public road—

Tho there is rarely anyone here to see me
No traffic I wish to pedal firmly not slowly

Neither aged nor unduly athletic. The river meets
The road once more after the latter runs down from the hill

& usually, here, I am pleased to give myself up again
To my own thought—about my daughter my self

My past—that is where I sometimes see
The beavers, where yesterday the cyclist

Whom I usually see on my trip out, in
His black & blue,

Is having a picnic. So I call out. "Good day to you!"
But no, I see he is repairing a puncture—he has

The wheel off & the tube is out
& he is squeezing it, where the glue is drying, between

Thumb & forefinger. He waves to me with his other hand.
I spoke to him once, as we rode,

About his studies. I told him about my daughter.
There's the beaver, climbing out.

I have a special affection for this young man
For a long time I suspected he was the one

My daughter was talking of—that he might not know
He was conversing with the mother of his girlfriend—

I grew quite to like him
& now he can cause me no trouble I like him even better

On A Page Beginning "Dear Laurie"

"Dear Laurie,"

late at night
in a bright light
I am beside a sleeping other

the night seeming endless, pleasantly—

only their breathing for sound

A slight ringing
in my ears
is the silence,

the bed clothes
rustle
once or twice

Consciousness
seems
the *only* pleasure,

the gift of
being here —

Will I stay up all
night?

& in my notebook

I find this poem,
dedicated to you —

Why, Kenneth Clark?

for Laurie Duggan

Watteau's happy people make us cry.
They do not see what surrounds them —

Time, & a lot of
big trees, fugitive sky.

What is it that
they are looking at
instead,

these departees for Cythera,
these abashed, nonplussed or charmed
hangers-about? Don't they see?

Still, better than television.

We feel sorry for them—
an ideal—when up & down the street
— this street here,
any street anywhere —
are people taking in
the various little abnerisms
propounded by *The Dukes Of Hazzard!*
Why, Kenneth Clark?

actually I could 'go'
as Dad would say
a little *Dukes Of Hazzard* —
                right now,
say 15 minutes worth
followed by a totally formulaic
70s detective show,
undistinguished, *almost*

for preference — but instead I read
The Religious Life Of Samuel Johnson.

I could go
down the back,
pinch one of
Tom's cigarettes,
& play James Brown
               — one of the
Live at the Apollo sets

How to explain
to Samuel Johnson
the thrill & special intensity
of James Brown?
demonstrate
the dance steps — some of
them — the twirls & spins
the one-leg shuffle across the stage,
               the time
Crab tried it in the
Westbury Street kitchen,
& nearly crashed thru the wall
broke a louvre in the window —
that we had to hide from Mary?
Johnson could explain to me
the efficacy of prayer. This guy,
who wrote on Johnson, could explain *nothing.*
Still.   Hullo Laurie

People Passing Time (Larry D mix)

— at the spectacle   probably
          — *in the other pic* —
          — something moving
              —books

                                      as alive
                                    - *Sleep*
                                  - tho it sounds
                                 -'Very funny'.
                              "got a drawing to do"
                  & Half aghast
                              & I cannot hesitate
                  & I've
              & not too cute
& now I've done this drawing
                                      & passing time
                              & the scribble I've added, left,
                          & this contemporary detritus
                                      (- could Life
(after all, this may happen to you
          (or Baroque)
          (the curtain) —
                      … but I won't
                      …   Late at night
          a cup   a yoghurt container —
                      a rounded cartoon in profile
                          about John, the poet, 'from the
  About to snap one down,
                                  against the dark blue
against her face
an old tape
Anyway,
as always   —
                              As are the girls
as Brecht & Eisler said

                                                            As is
Guston
                              As is Muddy
                                              at a ceiling,   at his life ...
                                      at the movies
attention to it   meaning
Attitudes to life
azure blue

                                                                    'be'
'Bernini'
                                              best
better that way
biro caps
blowing gum.   Life.   God, I'm glad I live in a century
bon mots
                                      bored,
                        Boredom,
Brilliantly lit

                                                              but
but I don't care
But not me yet
by the way
                                              composed   on his bed
contemplating
                              considered as a problem
                                      consolation
              Dead or dying
                                      dead too
death
                                                      'desk furniture'
                              disfiguring the poem
                        does drawing.
                        Don't you
dozing
eyes wide, smoking

fixes it.
for Micky Allan
get the idea

            Gig's? Laurie's?   Mine, maybe,
               girl puts knuckles in
            God, this will bring me down.

got the main girl right
grave' etc

                        her mouth

his mind?

          His speaks to mine

                  his supply of

       His was alive

                I am like the girl now,

I hear John say from the grave

               I say I've

I wonder whose voice said those things to John

              I'm alive.

    I'm on my way to Denver

                     in

In a *world* of trouble   says Joe.

           in the pic John wrote

about

          Intelligent appraisal

      is okay

            is *this* any good?

    it occurs to me to say something

             It shows the Five

Basic
It's too late, too late—

         I've pronounced that

"motts"

    I've tried everything I could / just to get along with
               you

jars of pencils
Jesus,

Joe Turner said that.

John who is dead

John, forgive me for being a jerk

just as I've disfigured the drawing

like a very quiet limb

like John was

Like my last

'live' "For Sentimental Reasons".

lying on each other, blowing gum,

maybe, to write to Laurie

Micky,

migrant

mine was asleep

More comforting than lovely

Muddy Waters

music

My

Nearer,

New Yorkers

nor did he, maybe

Not that there's any point

O sky of streaming

of Adult Life

of the curtains

on occasion.

On the wall

opinion)

over

pencil cases I never open

photographed   by Weegee

photographed in 1942

picture of John

pictures of people passing time

playing cards

presented to them

probably

                    protection
Rapt attention,

                                        really horrible

saying it now

          singing

                                    Sleeping,
              smiling

                    so *Mean?*)

So my time passed
some classical allusion

                    staring sightless

                                        that fill the rest.

that has collected against the window ledge.
that resembles the Guston

                                    The basic attitude.
                                    The fluoro desk lamp
                                    The 'late' Sam Cooke is

the main girl
the mess of papers, folders

                        The others are just shapes, but you
                    their human, evaluating faces
              Tho *I* didn't think he would die

                        tho they drape mostly

                                        Time,

                                    to have an

                              'Too cute!'

          Too late   too late   too late

                        transfixed

              was amazing

                              watch, toothpicks

          What would a *similar* shading be   for the poem—
when I sit back   makes a great white diagonal
Where

              Where

                        Where, will you *be* tonight ?

Which drape like *Renaissance* drapery

which was given me upon earth

who has painted his own head

with electric light.

Young girls

Outdoor Pig-keeping, 1954 & My Other Books on Pigs

Pig Farming. Methods Of
was a book I wrote in 1945
tho what I knew then of
pig farming you may wonder. It is
a human enough activity.
I mean 'universal'—did they have
pigs on Easter Island, the New Guinea
highlands, did the Maori? *Virgil*
knew about pigs, tho I associate him, more,
with bees, my Latin education centering
on a limited number of texts—
bits of *Caesar's Gallic Wars*
or *Punic Wars* ("Carthage delenda est"?)—
& not much else. Virgil. Ideas of
pig farming might be innate. (?)
Where do correct ideas come from?
"The head, boss." Pigs pretty much
know what they want (isn't that
often thought to be the problem,
the thing held against them?),
give it to them. "Long pig" was somehow
special dark knowledge when I was
a schoolboy, I mean the term.
A human dish. (No one else ate it,
except the odd lion or tiger—
as a one-off: humans also
protect their own—better probably not
to eat them too often.) But, to return
to the term, "long pig" implies knowledge
of "pig plain" sure enough. It seemed
insulting, to me, back then—to the idea
of the human & humanity & I didn't like

to utter it. I remember once
someone telling me of an abandoned
hippy farm where they'd been producing
heroin. The pigs were fed
on scraps & excrement
& were squealing. Addicted.
Apparently the noise was horrible. I did,
at some time, sleep near where a pig
——or pigs——squealed all night. I can't remember
now whether it was simply very affecting
or whether it was specifically because it sounded
human. It was loud, incessant & frightened.
I can't remember where or when. An
abattoir. In 1945
I had not read Virgil. I do know that.
It seems we've passed this way before. In
'another life' I may have *been* a pig farmer:
I see me, late at night at a plain kitchen table
writing *Pig Farming, Methods Of*. It's
electric light——tho it could do with a stronger
bulb. I write it in a child's school exercise book.
My only daughter has died? It's hers, hardly used,
& I turn it round & start at the back?——or maybe
continue right on from where she left off.
She had been studying & had written *amo, amas,*
amat etc. The vocabulary list begins with
"agricola"——farmer. As I see it the farmer
does not become especially sentimental about
the exercise book. He may have done, must
have done, at some time since his daughter's death,
but now he writes. Perhaps he writes with
extra care because it is her book. Perhaps he writes
because it is her book. He has not written
anything else before. He writes now
because she is gone. She was the future
& he was content to work to see her through——

to her adult life. But now she is gone
he must make something else. He is a widower.
I was brought up by my own father,
alone, me & my sister. We kept dogs & cats
& pigeons, a horse. No pigs. Anyway,
there it is, & it has my name on it, 1945—*Pig Farming,*
Methods Of.

Same Bed — Small World

I'm listening to Lyn Hope's band *("Tondalayo"*
and *"Eleven Til Two")*. Earlier, Joe Turner
and Crab's Cocktail Hour — heroes
of warmth and generosity. Late at night
— morning — reading a young New
Zealander and an old New York poet, tho
stuff he wrote at a similar age,
the one innocent, sad and full of yearning,
the other worldly, bitter and distant from his feelings
though attuned to them perfectly. I am
close to my feelings tho not attuned to them
not very innocent, not very worldly,
unhappy mostly tho of a sunny disposition.
People are never as interesting as one's
idea of them — tho since I know so few
I remain interested. A sort of social solipsism.
I read the New Yorker's art criticism
this week. Very good — fun, intelligent.
This morning I woke crying — a dream
of Crab's wake: in the dream I explain to someone at a
nightclub, after all the ways it might have come,
how it was an accident — electrocuted —
in my dream I see a hand plug something into a socket
— "What am I going to do?" I say and begin to cry.
I wake up. It takes a while to be sure
this is not part of my real knowledge. Crab
is alive. Playing tonight at the Cargo Club.
But real tears.

Some nights & days

I can hear
        rain on the roof
                scattered windy gusts

of it, till it becomes
        more steady.
                This means I cannot go

& look at the moon—
        which I saw
                last night,

looking full,
        as I rode home,
                the same day I had read

in the Larkin biography
        something about how, older,
                you look at it & it means

much less than it did
        but which
                it *still* means

to someone, somewhere. To me
        it can always look any of—great
                sharp, pitiless, hard, rocky,

soft—piercingly sad, charmingly—
        butteredly—cheering & optimistic
                sometimes at the same time

sometimes not—but the repertoire
        of identifications comes up

regularly

none have ceased
                to be available
                        or to take their turn.

Like a favourite record, or CD.

I wonder
                if I am the first
                        to compare the moon to a CD.   Hm.

In a minute I will make a
                cup of tea & banana sandwich.

                The moon looks far better

than a CD, of course. Another pioneering
                phrase! I am not so young that they
                        have, for me, much emotional impact—the sight

of them, I mean—like records have—tho that too
                has begun to drain away, with the knowledge
                        they will disappear—Sand collapsing down

the neck of an hourglass.

                — *As* the time for vinyl
                        starts running out, the black disks

begin to look like *old technology,*
                less like miracles.

                Christ, what
a way to spell "miracles"! (Fixes
                mistake)

Well,

now I can go & look at the moon. (The

rain has stopped.) —Though, I guess I won't.

I once wrote a poem about

smoke? cloud? fog?

pressing against my windows

as it began to grow light: I don't think

I was ever sure what the phenomenon was.

And I wrote the poem in stanzas of

three lines the second of each

being the second line of one of

the poems I had chosen randomly

from a poet I liked. It was

a loopy procedure—a 'mediating device'—

thru which to apprehend the reality

outside, though I liked the result. I remember

the room I wrote it in—

or the two rooms—the kitchen & lounge room—

in one of which I wrote it—the latter,

I'm sure. "Just write great first lines—an

endless rolling, of smoke across my window"

was how it began. I think. First lines

never were my specialty. Though one more

good line wouldn't hurt—& why not

the first? The newspaper TV program

across which is the pad I'm writing on

features the by-line photograph of a columnist—

taken from below, so he stares out

        above one, over one's head, with 'far-seeing eyes'

                the whacker—he must've done it deliberately

as no other columnist would, certainly

        none of the women, & the guy across from him,

                Errol Simper, seems simply concerned

to annihilate

        the associations of his name (he looks

                a Hollywood Nazi—grim, grim, grim).

The other (the 'idiot')

        is Phillip Adams.

                I read the column: *it*

is idiotic too—anything but visionary

        or even thoughtful—about pirates! I decide

                to read the Simper. From experience (I occasionally

do read him) I know it will be more densely argued.

        (Again, the problem—the spur of the name.) I wonder

                what he says? I read it—or begin—& realize

I did read it,

        just a few minutes previously.

        The wind is blowing outside now

hard & rainless—a door or window

        rattles occasionally, & a piece of tin makes that

                'billowing' sound. The trees register the wind

constantly, as if, beyond the glass,

        they are under water: shrubs the light from

this room catches bend & rock in a way

that seems 'troubled'—like autistic rocking—though
with plants we don't mind we can enjoy
our attributions, or give in to them—

feel sorry for ourselves, fretful & worried
or simply safe to be indoors. (That's something
I did right—stayed inside!) There is a letter

to Miriel to write, letters to others, too. There is
the Journal, of this nut, Allen Ginsberg. I tried
to ring Sal this morning—got Jane

instead—Pam & Jane's number just below hers
in my address book—I couldn't tell what was
happening. Luckily Jane knew my voice, so

we talked. Then I rang Sal:
& talked to her answering machine.
Pam rang earlier tonight.

One effect

of working so full time is
that hours of work-time go past & I can
hardly remember them, even 15 minutes after

Instead, my life seems to consist only of those
moments 'outside'—so, recalling the last few days
I can remember the fact that I went to work—

& mostly writing these letters, & *thinking* while I write
them—brief moments at the coffee shop
before work or at lunch hour (half-hour) — &

drinks with Crab tonight. Is this the Life Of The
  Mind?
     Is it, huh?

     Crab is told by
  John McConchie "not to be Utopian" in response
     to his complaint about ... his work situation (what

is it?—don't ask) as if to complain
  signals complicity with something
     worse than what one complains against. Mc

Conchie / is / "Wrong Again". So the space between
  writing to Becky, the calls to Pam, the *letter* to Pam,
     Kurt's arrival (I speak to *his* answering machine, too)

& this morning—where in 20 minutes at the coffee shop
  I look at mail: poems sent (& stories)
     & make my editor's note on their envelopes "No,
        merely" & "No, but

read again"—is telescoped: is my life being freezedried
  by one in another Universe,
     is this how you feel

as a coffee bean
  becoming Instant Coffee?

     I am so drunk, from drinking with Crabby,

I decide
  to stop writing.
     Now, I read the Robert Pincus-Witten

Review, a reprise of his 'time' at *Artforum*.
  — With different allegiances, with a different

version of his allegiances (only the names

have been changed), I would feel *I* was portrayed—I say *Yes,*
"in a way. Yes." But, I dislike, or am already distanced
from, some of his evaluations—Yes, I am similarly
placed,

vis a vis similarly placed oppositions   (tho something is
forgotten . . .
etc etc

quibble quibble)

Apparently I am not
Robert Pincus-Witten.

Surprise! —

Anyway, I don't write to Miriel,
I write to Becky, or try to. I am too tired. Tonight
I am too pissed. I write this instead.

For various movie directors

I come this way
for the 'S' bends
Driving alone at
night I feel
like Paul Douglas in a
wordy, moralistic
movie the kind
I loved—still do—
when I was young
these made
adulthood seem so
interestingly full—
of worries,
& heroism:
love, & guilt
& betrayal, unspoken
forgiveness: Paul always
loved her though she was
no good—though she wasn't
so bad—he was no
great shakes himself the
big palooka
besides, he had cancer,
his partner was out
to blackmail him
the business could go downhill
any moment—she'd given up a lot
to marry him. Paul wore
big coats, over big suits, &
sported a muffler he had
dumb, intelligent eyes. I
come home on just
one glass of wine, to play
an obscure record, write

a poem—obscure too probably—
write a letter
& maybe call Cath, in Italy—
on her holiday. Soon to return—
to her palooka, deeply worried
today, about Manet,
deeply worried about nothing—
a palooka in 1992 Australia
in a small yellow Mazda
moving carefully through the
'S's

Venetian

> "Pellucid stars chart my direction, you who
> never hear our intent or voices
>
> . . .
>
>   … yet as you
> are, I am."
>
>   —John Forbes

I seem to be at
some significant juncture—

what is it?

But the stars
roll into place,

whatever it is
they mean,

—turning
"in varied

impressive order".

Here at Pam's again,
reading Laurie's latest—

reading, tomorrow, a poem
that addresses John—

dead a year
at the time I wrote it.

Further down the track now:

the night still—
the traffic

rolling past—
Joe Turner's

song, "So long,
I hate to see you go"

heard
in a record shop today—

a kind of happily mournful
salute—derived from

Woody Guthrie's
'farewell'.

        The blinds
in the front room

cast a grid
of shadow—slim

parallel lines—on
the wall & open door—

              "Bad Boy"
the Eric Fischl painting—

tho here they carry
only the charge

of being adult,
sophisticated—

an association
from 40s film

                    A
*street*light?—or the
moon—throwing

that light?—

that lands, in thin
bars, silverly,

on wall, door, door
handle—the

latter rendered bright.

Further in to that room,
a dark square on a dark wall—

a painting by Buzzacott:
the early

modern period
Laurie's book

talks about—

a decade—*my* guess—
before the 'adult' image

of the venetian blinds.

'Time', I suppose:

the dead friend;
& this trip—

that *marks* time;

... the other poem
that I will read—

read *here*, amongst
these same tables &

chairs, years ago—

(about Cath, back home, about
her sitting in bed

reading
with Anna, with me).

What changes?

The stars say I age,
must say so

But, tonight, do I care?

The View at Sal's, David's

for Laurie in Brisbane

Dear Laurie,
          I'm writing this
from Sal's place—
& so looking
at something like the view
you used to have
(& miss a bit probably—
you got your new book
written there). Tho
you might be relieved
to be gone:
some views—even
great ones—paralyse.
Or is that me, only, who
has that reaction? Actually,
this harbour—& what it
stands for, as idea—
stymies me, more than
the specific view.

Anyway, here I am, writing.

I'm reading your book—
right now more or less—
& finding it enjoyable:
in no way dull.   Am
reading also your poems. (On these
more later.)

The view
is just right for your book—
so twenties,
& modern, or moderne
(tho understatedly)—the two palms
sticking their heads up into the harbour
the small sailcraft, tethered
their masts unexpectedly tall & spindly.
All of them face
directly at me
as I look at them. Very still:
the combo of massed foliage
that, at the bottom of the view

(the bottom of the window)—blocks out
the foreshore—& among it
suburban orange rooves.
If I move my head
I see, further on the right, the
high-rise that says *sixties,*
seventies, eighties. Too
tall for the first. Early
eighties maybe.

     Weirdly,
having faced me all day,
the boats are pointed now
to those buildings on the right,
the towers in fact
in one of which
you & Rosemary lived.

       I've read
your poems, the new ones, &
like them a lot but have not had time
to comment—not just that I'm busy
(am I?)—but that I can't open them
on my screen, except unformatted.
To read them properly
I must print them out.

     The
light has changed—
just suddenly, the way you'll
remember—the blue
in the one blue
patch of sky
suddenly silvering
—& the boats I think
have swung again
on their anchors—& in a second
it will go dark.
We're going out to dinner

Sal David Alathea Sarah
Pam & Jane. Japanese.

*

When I was
a teenager—I remembered last night—
I thought flats like the one you lived in
looked beautiful, & still do think that.
I had remembered that okay but had
forgotten the thoughts they used engender,
as I dreamed before them, in the train,
across the bridge to suburbia: the implied
shape of the building in the night
suggested, by its irregular grid
of orange-bright windows, a
busy de stijl. These glowing orange
rectangles seemed a kind of luxurious
fruit salad

warm & social—& 'modern' like
the venetian blinds. Catching the train
in the daytime, going from suburbs to
city (& to University), you saw those blinds
& imagined sophisticated infidelity—
women in slips (holding glasses, smoking,
talking to a man in bed); a man
helping a woman out of a bra. My dear young mind's
idea of romance.
                              One of the buildings
I see here tonight presents a vertical
cone of light—unbroken. (It must be
the stairwell; every floor alight, each unit
of brightness darkening
in the bottom left & right
corners. Reminding me, always,
of an x-rayed spine, or a picture I saw once
of a mosquito's heart—a line of interconnected
chambers that ran
most of the length of the insect—
like a tower of golf tees.)
Thoughts I have not had in decades.

                              May Gibbs'
keeping the bridge out of sight
I like. It *is* too big a gesture.
You report that she said this.
She kept it
relegated to her
peripheral vision, her studio slanted
to see just the rest
of the harbour—
so you say somewhere in your book.
It is funny to be focusing
on this tight view of Sydney
—Sal's view, your *old* view—

of a patch of harbour, boats, those
two weird islands—
Shark & Basket?—
while lying here,
finishing this letter,
a month later, in a bed
in John Jenkins'—where the view
is country, a high, near horizon
of arced rolling hills
morning mist—& trees—
viewed past nearby lavender. The
Japanese dinner was very pleasant
Alathea Vavasour & Sarah Kenderdine
know each other from Wellington.
(Sarah knows 'our' New Zealanders,
Greg & Jen.) As Pam said on the night,
It must feel good—surrounded
at the table by good looking women. (Who
can deny it?) Hanging round with Shan
& John has been nice—tho the social side
of Melbourne literature I'd run a mile to avoid:
a meeting to rue a magazine editor's
passing—passing from the job, not life—
& poets who talked of nothing but prizes,
their idea of their ranking, their next book's
chances. Unlucky encounters—that
you'd have dodged.

Tho Brisbane, I think, is *too far*

Not why you're there, I know.
Why am I here—or why
are we not all somewhere together?
Maybe life would be weirdly uneventful
minus the grit of its difficulties,
the sadnesses & beauties of its

perspectives—Sal, exotic in Sydney, you
& Rosemary a particular inflection of modern
in Brisbane, me, wrong about things generally
but happier maybe muddled than clear—

it seems sometimes, doesn't it?

I read allright, finally, in Melbourne—to an
audience (mostly) of young poets & crazies—Gig,
Brendan, Chris, Lauren Williams & others. Judith
Rodriguez showed up. The regulars, mostly, on
medication: shy, trembling loons (who, nearly all,
had something interesting to say—as opposed to
the merely 'bad' poets.) I wonder how interesting *I* was?
I mean—'really'? For a second, of course, I thought so.

A postcard Alan Wearne sent me

Well, he sent me many, over the years —
but this one I like a lot & found
again, recently, & it's in view, I
can see it now
from where I sit: a still
from an old Australian
movie called *Let*
George Do It
& George is lying on his back
on a diving board, fully dressed.
His feet are at the end
near the pool's edge —
so it looks for a second
as if he is levitating
out over the water
a few feet below. A posh
young woman — long, flared
dress — is saying *Eeck* or
George, you fool & some toffs
near her look at him & laugh. His
head is raised — comically —
to address them. He looks like
Anthony Quinn — why? how? —
but is George Wallace.
1938.
I've never seen the film
& maybe not George Wallace.
It's Australian:
'daggy' *avant la lettre*
(as we say now). Thank you,
Alan. How's things?

(THE) KIRKMAN GUIDE
TO THE BARS OF EUROPE

Kirkman Guide To The Bars Of Europe
their music, their service, views etcetera

Tony Kirkman—What are you doing here? Shouldn't you be in Europe?
Me—I'm going, I'm going. Next week.
Tony Kirkman—Tell us about the bars!

for Barbara & Tony

The Kirkman Guide
to the bars of Europe
begins in that city so
very much at Europe's centre—
though like the perfect bar,
where foot traffic is permitted
but not the noise of cars—not
too vertiginously at the
absolute centre
of the working world, not
London, Paris or Berlin—
which, though not like bars,
host many bars themselves—
but Rome. And where better
than the raffish, the louche,
the frankly insouciant Bar
San Calisto?

Nowhere, that's where! Dubious,
but confident, seedy but nonchalant,
the Bar San Calisto
issues its challenge.

What to have there? A Strega. And,
yes, we could consider the bars of Europe thus:
the best drinks—

& where to have them? A Cynar
in The Ghetto Bar of Trieste, a whiskey sour
in Prague's amusing Lucerna Cafe,
an ouzo at Madrid's Chicote, or the
Bar Cock. A retsina—
but you can only get those
in Greece... Or Australia.
Australia
is not Europe. Is Greece? We're thinking
'continental' Europe. Old World charm.
But if Prague, & London,
Edinburgh,
Cork & Dublin—why not Greece? A toast,
on Ithaka—or is it Hydra?—
to the Johnstons!

The Calisto is not the bar for everyone.
Is it too ricketty & ephemeral? Can
a celebrity *sit* there? No. The
San Calisto refuses the look extended, say,
by Harry's Bar, once, The Bar Americain—
for your Hemingway, your Robbie Williams,
for your Nick Cave, your Adam Cullen—
too real for one generic type, not
real enough for the other. Existential.
The San Calisto has
no 'amplifying' effect
for the personality that might require it—
Ashley Crawford? Robert Gray?
                    #
Ah, a sunny morning at the Bar San Calisto!
                    #
Outside the Bar San Calisto in the early evening
        chill.

A moment ago it was dusk, people drifted

from the square, hurrying home. Now, an hour
or so later, those out for dinner,
or a drink at a bar, throng the square—
& stare, some of them, at you.
Ripped. None of them comes
to the San Calisto, so stern its charm.
You drink on alone while inside a vocal
cohort of drunks shout & laugh, bathed
in its light. Better for you to sit tight—
tight in one sense & tight in the other—
&, because of this, plan your next move
with caution. Another inch of Strega
could be incapacitating
& you should get home. Deep breaths
(the advice of Johnny J)
seem both refreshing, in the cool,
& giddy-making. The voyage will be
a test & an adventure. Another afternoon
at the San Calisto.

      I have to laugh.
Laurie at the San Calisto? But no Internet,
no jukebox! Pam?
Pam would find its sham quality
'de trop'. Gig? Too self conscious—
fearing to appear 'taken in'. Peter B. on the other
   hand,
likes it, I know. And I can see him there—
see him only in my 'mind's eye'—
but he 'resembles' there
the same Peter we see everywhere,
even in Melbourne—so my
mind's eye's view is accurate!
He wears a hat or maybe a beret
& reads the film criticism, say,
of Manny Farber—as you would

at the San Calisto. John Tranter,
another major poet, sits quite near,
oblivious, having a Campari Soda, a good drink
to have at the Calisto. "Tranter!" says Lyn T,
who has just entered, & looms in the doorway,
"So this is where you are! What a dump!" Peter Bakowski
frowns.

David Kennedy, dressed a little like
Richard Harris in *This Sporting Life*,
though benign, benign, sits in
the San Calisto. What does he read?
Who knows? Perhaps he is marking
essays. But no—he would not bring work
to the San Calisto. I might.
I do. But then, I'm that kind of loon.
I buy David another beer,
a Guinness, not the 'usual thing'
at the Bar San Calisto, but he is
my English friend & I want him in character.

Orson Welles. I see the Harry Lime figure.
Authentic? In-authentic? Neither.
It was not the point. *That* is
the Bar San Calisto's attitude. Is
the Bar San Calisto authentic? Are you
kidding? Is it not? Sure it isn't. It is
the Bar San Calisto—"just as you left it".
(I think the Welles figure was Alan Wearne.
I have been astral travelling.) It is
the Bar San Calisto— just as you left it.
Someone has swept. So the butt-ends
are not embarrassingly in the way, the 'offing'.
It is itself almost detritus. If Italy
would only clean up its act it would be gone!
Is that fair to say? It may be true.

Berlin has no San Calisto. A San Calisto in Britain—
fashionable for fifteen minutes.
Then people would move on.
Used up. In Paris it would become
dowdy, or sad—& upgrade
& succeed at being something else,
the bar Borgelt or Bougogne
or something suggestive
of new cars & insurance. The Bar San Calisto—
the real one, in Rome, exists. Is it 'a Gilligan
among bars'? No, Steve. (Steve Kelen.) *No,* its clientele objects
(some, apparently, care), *It is not sappy.* So who, what?
Watteau's *Gilles,* Stan Laurel? No. Yes. I don't know.
Could you repeat the question?

But having bought it—did I buy this?—Kennedy may have
bought it, or Tranter. I see that they are gone. A Cynar,
or a three inch yellow Strega—where will you
sit, inside or out? That is the problem, not such a
bad problem. Where will you sit in the San Calisto—
time passing differently in each reality,
inside & out—where? It would be good to sit
with Ava Gardner, outside, or Johnny Depp. But inside:
it would be terrible. It is always terrible to sit
inside—a hell interminable—& which every minute
calls for all your attention—
the sort of thing, probably, Sartre hated, though it
puts you on your mettle. Are you tough enough
for the San Calisto? You look at the photo
someone has pasted up, of Howlin' Wolf
hunched forward, boxing gloves raised
& full of menace—
or the neighboring photo of Muhammad Ali
fronting Howlin' Wolf's band—plainly
a switch has been made—& the existential
threat, the challenge, is terrific.

I remember someone—crazy Robert Hughes?—
characterized the bar Van Gogh drank in
as a place where "a man could go mad". The
Bar San Calisto? Yes, it is maddening. (Women will note
It is always "a man".) Something
has occurred to me, that
has occurred to me before—days, minutes ago?—it
reminds me slightly of the fly-paper,
the hopeless futility of it. An each-way bet.
Did it catch flies, attached there, hanging,
from the fan of the San Calisto? The futility—
death, death, death! Some have died, stuck to the shellac.
Some haven't, slowly spinning, in the wind from the fan,
where Howlin' Wolf, Muhammed Ali, Joe Louis
challenge one & the table needed something additional
shoved under one leg to make it balance—
a bit of ear would do it—& the bicycle racing team
or soccer team from 1974,
combative, implacable, somehow raise the ante
& an old woman comes in, sits down opposite, in black
& moments later you are outside the San Calisto
& stumbling from it, a foreigner, & it is good
to be a foreigner—to use Hemingway's formulation—
abashed, unnecessary, challenged—
like someone in *Fiesta*—but Australian,
because that is how you do things, as if the spirit
were an eye & the Calisto a burnt stick
poked in it—but the spirit is
better than this & you have learned something.

(Learned not to come back to the San Calisto
till you can claim, plausibly, to have forgotten
what took place here. So maybe not tomorrow.)

A bloated, inebriate Russel Crowe, an etherized,
botoxed Nicole Kidman. Emma Balfour. At the

San Calisto? Maybe. Emma, buy Nicole a toasted
sandwich. I might buy Ava one—or Anna
Banens-Kenneally: she looked real at the San Calisto.
I see her outside. Now. Hey, Frontein!

Does this guide mean to say
the San Calisto Bar is the only bar in Italy?
No, in Lecce, for example,
in the square, a number of pleasant
watering-holes abide & beckon. Further North,
in Trieste, the Ghetto Bar is a nice place to be,
pleasantly situated & drawing
a very nice crowd of friendly people.
One night I sank quite a number
of rather large Cynars there—
a curious drink to order at all
at that hour, perhaps, & in quantity, from
an Italian point of view. But
the Ghetto crowd were amused.

Cynar might constitute a sort of test case.
In Split the waiter refused
to acknowledge that he knew it—
"We have no Cynar—whatever that is!"—
though one's finger found it on the menu—
the same menu the waiter continued to put out
on all the tables. You can buy Cynar
at the Bar San Calisto.

In Berlin one longs to stand
proud & tough & worldly, like Beckmann
in his famous self-portrait, or slump,
debauched & frowzy, like Fassbinder—
which requires no suit or bow-tie, there is
that to be said for it—and drink good wine,
or whiskey. Berlin has come a long way, since

Laforgue's time. *He would hardly recognise it.*
(He would find it much improved,
though disconcertingly modernized.)
(By the same token, he would hardly recognize
Paris, either.) I look out the door of the
Alt Berlin, paradoxically a Negroni in my hand.

The Negroni is not such a great drink—
but it was mentioned often in the books of my youth,
that I read to develop sophistication,
so I try it. No, I cannot see the point.
A cowboy walks past, in modern Berlin—
the sort of outlandishness
Laforgue would deplore—would have—and I am
almost with him, on that, except
Dennis Hopper, in *The American Friend*, dressed that way,
a film set in Germany—
&, in the modern era—*pace* Laforgue, & in fact
who knows how Laforgue is dressed 'these days'?—
you can do this thing. This guy has.
I see with surprise, but not quite surprise,
it is Richard & Suzie.
Suzie is dressed strikingly—but 'normally'—& says,
"All this way, to Europe, to drink Negronis?"
Richard says, "Let me buy you another!
Or are you switching?" Noting my discomfort.
We place our orders. It is great to be in Berlin,
at Munz Strasse's Alt Berlin, with them,
myself again, not Max Beckmann.

#

On August Strasse is the Hackbarth,
for hanging out after openings, also
The Ballhaus Mitte, formerly of old
East Berlin, lovely front garden, with benches,

& upstairs an old & faded ballroom, with ornate mirrors
whose reflective powers are nil,
into which you may peer, glass in hand,
& wonder where your soul has left for, & will it
'return', will you be Audie Murphy when it does,
or Giorgio di Chirico, Zazu Pitts or Stendhal? John
        Meillon?
Can mirrors do that,
or only with enough Jameson's
famous Irish whiskey? Each glass is like the last
but tells you something different.

On Berlin's Karl Marx Allee is
Cafe Moskau. It caters to those
with a special nostalgia for the 'East'.
I have none—though I recently purchased
this pack of *Sprachloss* cigarettes. 'Speechless'
the name translates as, which I love
for its suggestion of emphysema,
the *Trabant* of cigarettes. I don't smoke
but I like the packet—like the
Ardath of my youth. Hip & expensive—
but if you can't resist the idea
of drinking in a former Czech or
East German travel agent's—
further down Karl Marx Allee is the CSA Bar.
What should you have? Stolychnaya, perhaps.
Or a Mickey Finn. Ha ha, the Cold War & its
Maxwell Smart ways.

Paris!—*speaking of spies*—a prosecco
or a Ricard at Le Varenne,
on Rue de Varenne,
where Harry Mathews lives.
A common sight—Mathews
drinking with his cryptic friend,

Georges Perec.

In Budapest, where I went in 1992:
I don't remember the name of the bar.
It was in a small cellar. The tables
were in vaulted stone arches. And it
was full of Hungarian intellectuals
in heated discussion. You can tell them from
Australian intellectuals by their tall
foreheads, but you can't tell them
this way from other Hungarians—
they all have the tall foreheads,
the rather fine features, the clear skin:
think chess, madness, manic depression.
I will have what they're having.

In Lisbon's Pavilhao Chines, on Rua Dom Pedro V,
the bar is full of curiosities—tin soldiers,
model trains, hats, model planes. The effect,
'paradoxically', is to force you upon yourself—
which is why I go to bars anyway
(Hullo, who are you? *It's me you fool,*
I've come back to claim you,
or to touch base at any rate—
haven't you had enough?)—
at Pavilhao Chines
there is the sudden urge
to dust, to order a drink,
sweep all the stuff into a sack
& clear off, before the drink comes.
Then you breathe out, you drink the drink
& go somewhere—the Mirador de Graca or Casa do Alentejo,
which are pretty, frankly,
& where you can have fun
& scuttle home, even late at night,
without too much hissing from the lecherous men

if you've become a woman, as maybe I have become
with all this drinking—Imogene Coca, Madeline Kahn,
Sarah Crowest, Thelma Todd. Vinho Verde
did this? Anyway, to quote my friend Dave Glazbrook,
"There's a little Audie Murphy
in every girl", & I check my knuckle-dusters
are in my purse, order
another wine, cast a final look
over the gardens, palm trees, moorish arches, the lemon
& olive trees that my heart loves so much,
toss back my drink & make my way out.
I push the waiter hard in the back
as I pass—now why did I do that—
he pulled my pigtails in another life? I start to run
as I hear the crash & cry of surprise,
back to my apartment in Mouraria
in lovely Lisbon. What a night!

The waiter, actually, looked like
Tony Kirkman! *Kirkman, you got me into this,*
asking for an account of the bars of Europe.
But *was* it Tony?

In Newcastle, England, there's the Bodega.
A grand old losers' club. I was talking to a trust-fund
Scandinavian artist there one night,
when who should walk in
but Suzie Treister. I bought her an Australian
white wine & we got along famously—me, Suzie, & Sven,
if that was his name. He had blonde hair & clear skin
& wore a polo-neck jumper.
His eyes were pale, & staring in them I could see
an horizon line, of snow, with little wolves
running from left to right. Then I realized
it was the reflection of the greyhound racing
on the bar's tv

& as Sven wasn't saying much I went outside with the Treister.

In London there is The French House in Dean St., Soho
& the Coach & Horses, in Greek Street, nearby.
Down Lamb's Conduit Lane there's a nice pub
& a nice Italian restaurant. In fact, London
is full of bars that are nice places to drink, though none,
sadly, is the San Calisto.

In Dublin—though do the Irish still drink?
I mean 'any more'? Did they ever?
Are you kidding? Does Derek Marnne?
Like a fish! But where? All over town!
Here & in Belfast. He is a man-of-the-world,
an international drinker—he actually *does*
look a little like Max Beckmann in his photographs—
  perhaps
he should be writing this!
      I *can't*—
or can I?—see him at the Bar San Calisto.

Notes

2.30—a night up late, writing. Alan Wearne had rung to tell me of Rae's birthday.

Letter To Akira—mentioned in passing: the Festival of Ideas—an Adelaide institution in which intellectuals & 'experts' are imported to think & debate before the public. Fiona Hall, a prominent South Australian artist, had a retrospective at the Art Gallery of South Australia at the time of the poem. Hornsby is a Sydney suburb. The "people you have to read now"—French Theory was mandatory (remains mandatory?) at the Art School. "The Simones": Simone de Beauvoir & Simone Signoret — but not, probably, Simone Simon.

Apollinaire—his grave, famously, is in Pere Lachaise, temporarily outshone by that of the Doors' Jim Morrison. "Amply repays the debt" ran some early praise from David Malouf—which, naturally, I have never forgotten.

Art History is nearly all art references. For the others: Gully Jimson is an artist character in Joyce Cary's novel *The Horse's Mouth*; Roy Rene was an Australian vaudeville comedian—much loved as the character 'Mo'.

Brisbane Letter to Gabe—mostly written while at the Brisbane Poetry Festival, to Gabe Banens in London.

Contretemps—begins with some lines from John Forbes. Thereafter, his friends, & I, are seen with him on the set of *The Honeymooners*, a 50s TV comedy.

Exotic Things—from the journal of a trip I made through Africa in 1962 with friends & my then wife Kay Kendall.

A Few Days recounts a day's activities. There is mention of a tape featuring two Adelaide bands Speedboat & Crab's Cocktail Hour—the latter a smaller spin-off from the other, drawing on the same personnel. Both were great.

Mary, Mill—Mary Christie & daughter Millie Dickins, the pair of them at the time teaching in Japan.

Monday, Hi Pam—full names of the artists referred to are Sarah CrowEST, Matthew Bradley, Christian Lock, Marg Dodd & Gerry Wedd & an artist called KAB-101

Odd Quartet—these poems took their energy—or permission—from reading the reliably stimulating—& terrific—Ron Padgett.

People Passing Time (the LD mix—Laurie Duggan's rigorous re-mix of a poem I wrote mourning, & addressing, John Forbes.

Outdoor Pig-keeping—idly checking my name on the Amazon site, I found one of my books listed—as well as one I didn't know about, on pig-keeping. Another Ken Bolton was out there.

Some nights & days—The opinions, about Errol Simper & Philip Adams, are they a little unreasonable?

Venetian Twins — two poems begun, about a year after John Forbes' death, back in Sydney at the apartments of friends—whom I'd last visited at the time of his funeral. Laurie Duggan had, by that time, left Sydney for Brisbane, though he is now further away in the UK. There is a reference to a book of his: it is *Ghost Nation*, a study of aspects of early Australian modernism. I began to finish the second poem at John Jenkins', outside Melbourne.

The Kirkman Guide — Some names herein are obscure or close to obscure—& funny maybe for being nearly lost: actresses like Imogene Coca, Thelma Todd, & actor, war-hero & prone to fight, Audie Murphy. Some friends' names are in the mix, especially those who supplied notes on bars. Frenchman Laforgue is mentioned for his cranky account of nineteenth-century Berlin.

Acknowledgements

Outdoor Pig-keeping appeared in *Best Australian Poems 2009* and
with Odd Quartet was published in *Heat*
For Various Movie Directors appeared in *The Famous Reporter*
Kirkman Guide in *Southerly* and *foam:e*
Luminous Hum in *Ekleksographia* and *Southerly*
Exotic Things was exhibited—as *Seven Exotic Things*—with
illustration by Vivienne Miller—at the CACSA Gallery in 2008